Best Wishes

CW01664884

THE SAMMY MILLER MUSEUMCOLLECTION

Racing and Sporting Machines

REDLINE BOOKS

THE SAMMY MILLER MUSEUM COLLECTION

Copyright Sammy Miller 2009
All rights reserved. Apart from any fair dealing for the purpose of private study, research, criticism or review, as permitted under the Copyright, Designs and Patents Act, 1988, no part of this publication may be reproduced, stored in a retrieval system, or transmitted in any form or by any means, electronic, electrical, chemical, mechanical, optical, photocopying, recording, or otherwise, without prior written permission. All enquiries should be addressed to the publisher.

ISBN: 978 0 9555278 0 7
Printed in England by Advent Colour

REDLINE BOOKS

Sammy Miller MBE.

There is no space here to detail every facet of Sammy Miller's astonishing career as motorcyclist, businessman and museum magnate, and indeed it has been described in biographies elsewhere. But this book, plus the sparkling exhibits in the Sammy Miller Museum, will serve to highlight many facets of his amazing motorcycling achievements. Sammy was born in Northern Ireland in 1933, and his future talents were forged during wartime schooldays in and around Belfast, when he and his friends frequented aircraft dumps garnering parts to make soap box carts, boats, and even a glider – his enthusiasm for aircraft still being seen in the model Junkers (shown opposite) suspended in his Museum. More significantly, his gang modified and repaired pedal cycles, and while racing them round rough tracks Sammy learnt many valuable lessons about machine preparation, balance and fitness. Starting his motorcycling career as a fifteen-year-old, Sammy was soon competing in grass track events and trials, and making a success of each. His Villiers/Matchless SH Special (see page 216) was the first evidence of his developmental skills, and his showing on it at the 1954 Scottish Six Days Trial led to the works ride for Ariel that began his twenty year domination of the trials scene. Meanwhile, Sammy had begun racing an AJS 7R – naturally represented in his museum – and his instant and unmistakable

Designed and published by Redline Books.
www.redlinebooks.co.uk

talent in that sphere led to him becoming a works rider for NSU and Mondial, showing world class on both marques. Deciding to concentrate solely on trials in the late 1950s, Sammy won literally hundreds of events and championships on his Ariel GOV 132 (see page 190) as he developed it into the most famous trialler ever, and afterwards he achieved the same success with Bultaco, Honda and SWM. Sammy's serious riding activities naturally began to tail off in the 1980s, but anyone who thought that he would fade into the background clearly didn't know their man. Alongside his already thriving business in special parts for modern and pre-65 trials machines, he threw more and more of his vast energy into his rapidly expanding Museum. Collecting, restoring, and demonstrating older motorcycles – especially those with a sporting or racing pedigree - has become a consuming passion for Sammy, and in 2009 his work earned him his MBE. Today his museum houses the country's foremost collection of such machines, many of them featured in these pages. This book will whet the appetite of those not fortunate enough to have already made a visit, and will provide a pleasant reminder for others until they come again.

Dear Sammy

My very grateful thanks for letting me see a set of proofs for the book.

I'm supposed to be good with words but, for once, they fail me. As you know my hobby is collecting motor sport books so, as an ex-advertising man with an eye for photography and layout, I can say with some experience that you've produced something that any enthusiast will be mighty proud to own. A wonderful record of a truly unique collection that is undoubtedly one of the best in the world.

We've known each other for a long time Sammy so I can say, with great sincerity that comes from the heart that, quite apart from the memories of your unmatched achievements in trials and racing, the world of motorcycling owes you an immense tribute for your enthusiasm, dedication and insistence on perfection which have masterminded your superb Museum and, now, this book.

In my opinion you ought to be Sir Sammy Miller rather than Sammy Miller MBE!

My warm regards and very sincere congratulations

Murray

Sammy Miller, Murray Walker and GOV 132 at Beaulieu Motor Museum

Contents:

BP
SHELL MOTOR SPIRIT
Esso
EXIT
SHELL MOTOR SPIRIT
Mobiloil
Redline
Mobiloil A
SHELL-MEX BP LTD
ROYAL SNOWDRIFT OIL
Royal Snowdrift
BOW BELLS
ROYAL DAYLIGHT OIL

www.sammymiller.co.uk

SAMMY MILLER MUSEUM

Bashley Cross Roads, New Milton, Hampshire, BH25 5SZ
Tel 01425 620777 Fax 01425 639407

1939 500cc AJS V-4

The magnificent AJS V-4 was probably the most ambitious racer ever produced by a British factory, and is one of the Museum's top exhibits. Always innovative and keen to gain publicity, the Wolverhampton manufacturer was among the first to progress to overhead camshaft engines, and in 1935 unveiled a sensational super-sports V-Four motorcycle with side-by-side pairs of light alloy cylinder barrels on a common crankcase, and overhead camshafts driven by a chain between the cylinders. These machines could be normally aspirated or supercharged, but were initially not especially successful in either guise. After another year of development the supercharged V-4 reappeared with plunger rear suspension, and showed potential but was limited by a tendency to overheat, a problem that was overcome in 1939, when water-cooling was introduced. In August that year it was ridden in the Ulster GP by Walter Rusk, and made its mark in the record books by becoming the first machine ever to lap a Grand Prix circuit at 100mph. Sadly that was the end of its career, as supercharged racers were banned after the war, and the Museum's restored example is the only genuine and complete AJS V-Four racer in the world.

Sammy at the Osterreichring, August 1993

1947
500cc AJS Porcupine Twin

After the difficulties encountered while developing the racing V-4, AJS's wartime planning for future GP racers centred on a simpler parallel twin with gear-driven overhead camshafts. Water-cooling was avoided by laying the new machine's cylinders flat to improve exposure to airflow, and this also lowered the centre of gravity and reduced the frontal area. Naturally the cooling fins were aligned with the airflow for maximum effect, and it was the spiky appearance of the cylinder head that gave rise to the racer's nickname of 'Porcupine'. Unfortunately, a new ruling from the sport's governing body meant that the engine could not be supercharged as intended, and so the machine could never show its full potential. Nevertheless, one – ridden by Jock West – set the fastest lap in the 1947 Senior TT until slowed by clutch trouble, and Les Graham would have won the same event in 1949, except for a failed magneto on the last lap. Greater success was found in other Grands Prix with Graham winning the 500cc Championship. In 1952 they redesigned the engine with the cylinders at 45 degrees and made many other modifications, thus creating the E95. The Museum's Porcupine is the world's only working example of this innovative machine.

Goodwood Festival of Speed, 2007

AJS
4

AJS
4

AERMACCHI
HARLEY-DAVIDSON

1967 Aermacchi Racer

Sammy on the Aermacchi with Walter Zeller, BMW, at Osterreichring, 1993

Before the Great War, Guilio Macchi set up in business in Varese, Italy, to make aircraft, and this gave his company its name. After WWII Aermacchi needed to diversify, and produced various lightweights, including overhead camshaft streamliners - designed by Lino Tonti - that set land speed records in 1956. Tonti was succeeded by Alfredo Bianchi whose task was to design a completely new motorcycle, the result being the futuristic semi-enclosed 174cc Chimera, which was soon followed by a 250cc version. Despite its good performance, the Chimera was not a saleroom success, but the tough pushrod engine was easily tuned, and the bodywork was simply removed, so it was soon being successfully raced in Italian sports-machine events. The factory followed the owners' lead, and in 1959 produced the over-the-counter 250cc Ala d'Oro (Golden Wing) production racer. The Museum's later and larger version was purchased from the late Albert Moule, a famous TT rider, and it benefits from engine improvements and a five-speed gearbox. Sammy Miller has used the Aermacchi in European Classic events, and says that although it is obviously not as fast as the Japanese factory racers, it is quick, reliable and very easy to ride.

1963 Aermacchi Ala D'Oro Production Racer

Over-the-counter racers were in very short supply in the early 1960s, and tuned versions of British roadsters were seldom competitive. Aermacchi thus filled a valuable market niche by removing the bodywork from the semi-enclosed Chimera to produce the Ala d'Oro (Golden Wing) in 1959. Because of its background it had a pressed-steel spine frame, and even more unusually for a racer, it had a pushrod ohv engine; designer Alfredo Bianchi arguing that that overhead cams were not required in a machine of this type. He was proved right, and the Ala d'Oro had a long and successful career, continuing in production until 1972, by which time many improvements had been introduced, and versions with capacities of up to 400cc had been developed. The Museum's example comes from quite early in the production run - just before Aermacchi gave the Ala d'Oro a five-speed gearbox and a short stroke engine - but despite this it gave 25bhp at 9000rpm, and its top speed was about 110mph. Interestingly - despite having developed the Ala d'Oro from a fairly unsuccessful roadster - Aermacchi went on to reverse history, and produced less highly tuned versions (including the well-known Ala Verde – Green Wing) for road use.

1938 AJS R7

AJS achieved great success in the Junior TTs of the early 1920s with overhead valve racers featuring the large exhaust pipe that led to the 'Big Port' nickname of the road-going derivative. This effectively began the factory policy of producing over-the-counter versions of factory racers. A new 350cc racer designated the K7 was introduced in 1927, featuring cutting-edge valve operation in the form of a chain-driven overhead camshaft. Although it showed promise, the machine was not instantly successful, and global economic conditions, plus a take-over by the rival Matchless concern, temporarily limited further factory participation and success in top-level racing. However, the ohc machine remained in production and was continually developed for both the works' riders and private owners. By 1938, when the Museum's example was made, the 350cc version of the machine had been re-designated the R7 (there was also a 500cc R10) and it featured further improvements including an aluminium alloy cylinder head. This is an ex-Works racer and features innovations such as magnesium alloy castings for the engine and gearbox, thus keeping the weight down to well below 300lb. Post war, the Model 7R continued the line of ohc racers available to the public.

1949 AJS 7R Boy Racer

Besides making more exotic factory racers, AJS produced the 350cc Model 7R to meet the demand for a tough and affordable racer that could be sold to the public. Introduced in 1947, the 7R was a relatively orthodox single cylinder machine with a bore and stroke of 74mm x 81mm, and a single camshaft driven by a chain on the right hand side. Only low octane 'pool' petrol was available at the time, and so the compression ratio was kept to 8.45:1, and the engine gave its peak power of about 30bhp at 7000rpm. It had a fairly narrow power band (partly resulting from its short, large diameter megaphone exhaust) but it was instantly popular with the works team and private owners. It was not overly successful at international level, with one of the best results being in the year that the Museum's machine was made, when works rider Bill Doran led the Junior TT until forced to retire near the end of the last lap. In private hands, however, the 7R proved to be one of the most popular over-the-counter racers ever, earning the affectionate nickname of 'Boy Racer' and being painstakingly developed until production ceased in 1962.

Cookstown winning ride, 1955

AJS

1954 BSA MC1

Doug Hele followed Bert Hopwood – the designer of the Norton Dominator – when he moved across Birmingham to the BSA factory at Small Heath. In return he was entrusted with the design of a radical new 250cc racer that could potentially form the basis of future production bikes. No expense was spared, and in 1954 Hele's unique design was unveiled. Its two carburettors and paired exhaust pipes made the complex overhead camshaft engine look as if it was a twin, but it actually had a single cylinder topped by two camshafts - interconnected by bevel gears - which operated four radially disposed valves each serving a separate port. The frame was equally innovatory, and the MC1 – as it was known – had Earles forks and cantilever rear suspension. It showed considerable promise, and in 1955 was due to be ridden at Aintree by Geoff Duke – the top rider of the day. Unfortunately, the Board of Directors got cold feet, and would not sanction the ride without a guarantee of success. Naturally, this could not be provided, so the unique machine was withdrawn from the race, and disappeared from sight, until rescued and restored for the Museum.

BSA

1951 Earles BSA

Ernie Earles was an important part of the post-war automotive scene in Birmingham, his Elms Metals Company producing pressings for neighbouring car and motorcycle manufacturers, while he ran a serious private motorcycle race team. During the war – while engaged on aircraft work – he'd become expert in the infant science of aluminium welding, and soon afterwards began making lightweight motorcycle frames, starting with an Ariel trialler. In 1951 he also devised a novel front suspension system - in essence a swinging fork pivoted from behind the wheel - that would overcome the obvious lack of rigidity in contemporary telescopic forks. All this came together in the Museum's gleaming machine, which is believed to be the one ridden by BSA employee Charlie Salt in the 1952 and 1953 Senior TTs. Its lightness is evident, as is the stiffness of its fully duplex frame, and it was still in fairly sound condition when acquired and restored in the mid-1980s. The roadster-based engine limited the machine's successes on the track, but it proved the worth of Ernie Earles' ideas with firms like MV Agusta and BMW adopting his design of forks, and aluminium frames now being accepted throughout the motorcycle world.

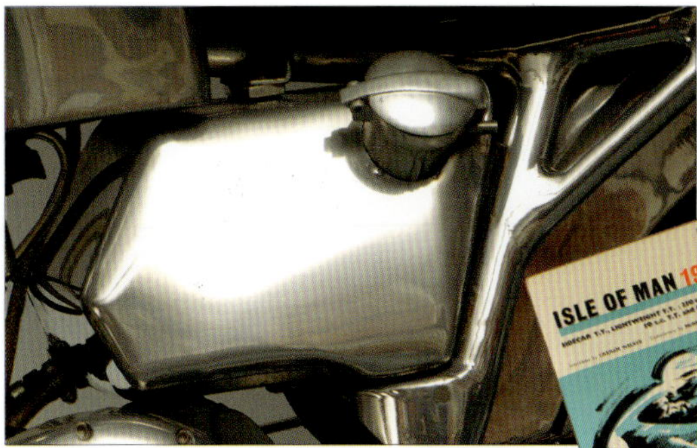

ISLE OF MAN 1962
TT
Sound Stories

1972 G50 Seeley Mk4

Colin Seeley came to prominence by winning the British Sidecar Championship in 1962 and 1963, driving an extremely smart home-built outfit powered by a Matchless G50 engine. That created a market for his frames, but rather surprisingly the greatest demand was from solo riders like Derek Minter who found that their straightforward, yet light and rigid structure provided superb handling. By the mid 1960s, the Associated Motorcycle Company was in terminal decline, and Seeley purchased the whole racing department including tools, drawings and spares. Soon, entire Seeley-Matchless and Seeley-AJS machines, including their G50 and 7R engines, were being made at the Belvedere, Kent works, and used by eminent riders including Tommy Robb, John Cooper and Mike Hailwood. Development continued, and in 1972 it resulted in machines like the Museum's five-speed G50-powered Mk 4 Seeley. The fairly conventional early frame had by now become even lighter and stiffer, with the engine suspended within a triangular structure that had dispensed with a conventional down-tube, and the all-up weight was reduced to well below 300lbs. Sadly, though, the private company could no longer compete with the Japanese giants at the top level and serious production ended in about 1972.

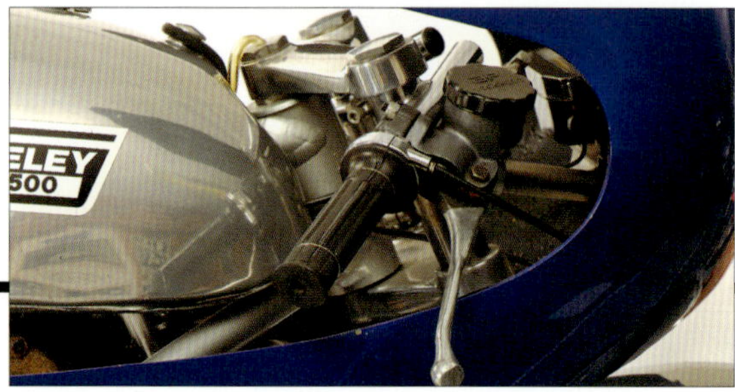

Sammy and Colin Seeley putting the world to rights

c1934
350cc Cotton-Blackburne Racer

The partially-triangulated frame of Francis Willoughby (Bill) Cotton's competition Scott inspired him to design a frame based on four straight tubes running between the steering head and the rear wheel spindle. He began manufacture in Gloucester in 1918, initially using Villiers engines, but later adding Blackburne, Python (Rudge) and Sturmey Archer-engined versions. Blackburne-powered Cottons were the most successful in competition, gaining First, Second and Third places in the 1926 Lightweight TT, and achieving much success at Brooklands in the hands of exponents like Eric Fernihough. The large petrol tank of the Museum's Cotton-Blackburne indicates that it was intended for use either in endurance speed record attempts at Brooklands, or long-distance races like the TT. It certainly has all the trappings of a serious racing bike, with practically everything drilled for lightness, a quick-action filler on the near-side of the oil tank, and an exotic magnesium-cased four speed Burman gearbox. This stunning machine goes as well as it looks, but it was almost the end of the line, as the triangulated frame did not lend itself to updating with rear suspension, and the original company faded out at the start of the war.

1965
250cc Cotton Telstar

The original Cotton Company faded out when the Ministry of Supply commandeered the Gloucestershire works during WWII, but the name was revived in the early 1950s by enthusiasts Pat Onions and Monty Denley, with the support of Elizabeth Cotton, the widow of the company's founder. Production initially centred on road machines using Villiers engines, but soon branched out into trials and scrambles bikes. And when Villiers launched its 250cc Starmaker competition engine, Cotton decided to re-enter road racing – the area in which it had made its mark before the war. With its mass-produced two-stroke engine, the resultant machine was never intended to be a world-beater, but it was a significant performer at club and National level. As the Museum's example shows, the Cotton Telstar (named after an early telecommunications satellite) was a well thought out machine with a simple, but light and rigid frame, and its Armstrong leading link forks gave excellent handling. It was particularly successful in the hands of Peter Inchley – already respected for his development of the Ariel Arrow two-stroke racer – and other well-known riders included Bill Ivy and Derek Minter. Cotton's racing involvement ceased when Villiers stopped supplying engines to other manufacturers.

Cotton
Telstar

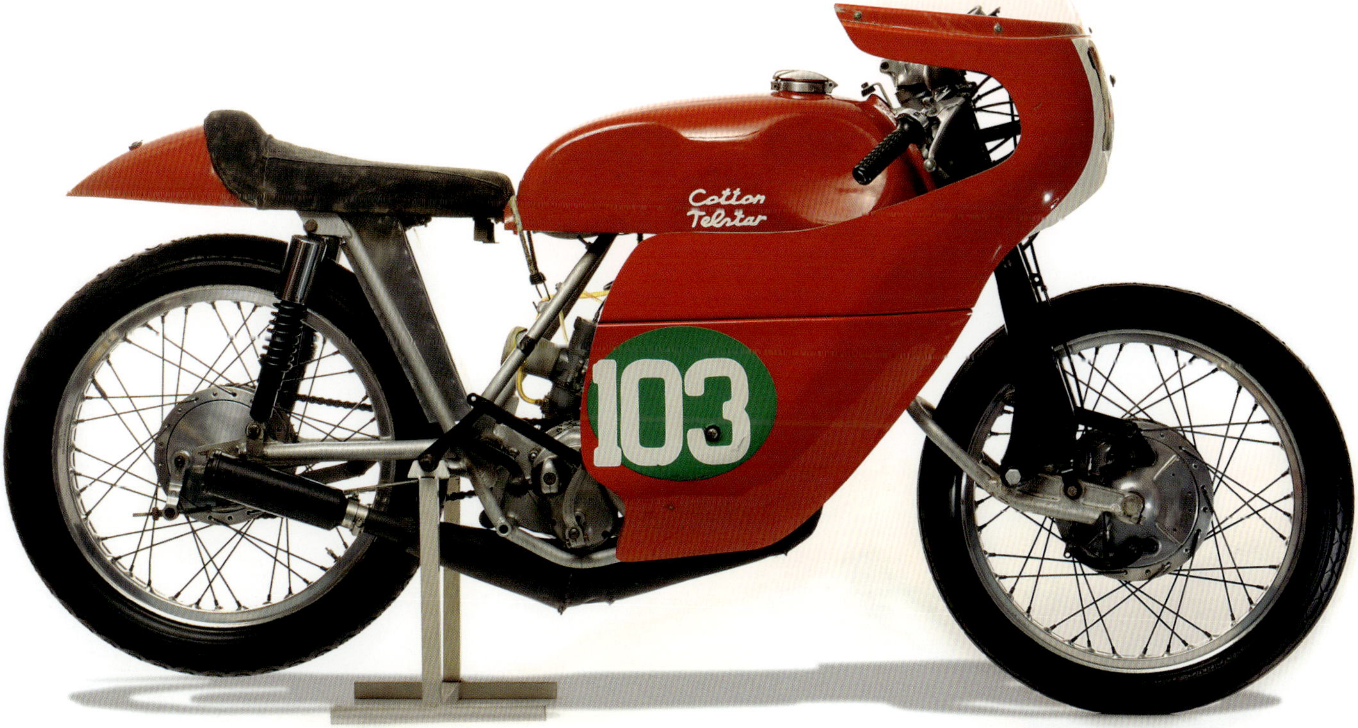
Cotton
Telstar
103

1930
350cc Face Cam Chater-Lea

The London-based company was founded by William Chater-Lea in about 1890 to make frame components, and by 1903 had graduated to making complete motorcycles with clip-on proprietary engines. Chater-Lea took an early interest in racing, and one of his machines came eighth in the 1908 TT. After WWI the firm achieved real prominence through its ace rider - Dougal Marchant - who in April 1924 used a Chater-Lea with a modified Blackburne engine to achieve the first 100mph lap of Brooklands by a 350cc machine. Many other successes were achieved there by Marchant, including that year's 200 mile 350cc sidecar race at a speed of over 60mph. Doubtless encouraged by this, Chater-Lea began developing its own engines, and in 1925 came up with the innovatory overhead camshaft design seen in the Museum. Instead of the usual camshaft running across the cylinder head, the cam's face is mounted on top of the vertical shaft drive, so that in operation it behaves rather like a miniaturised warped audio record. The machine never achieved the success that it perhaps deserved – it failed in both the 1927 and 1928 TTs - but it was a brave attempt to try something different.

1956
350cc Walter-CZ

Czechoslovakia's long motorcycling history would surprise those who only know the cheap two-strokes produced under communism. Josef Walter began making motorcycles in 1900, and in 1926 was joined by his sons Jan and Jaroslav in a new company. By 1939 Jaroslav Walter had created a successful 250cc ohc racer, and after the war he added a 350cc version of the unit construction, double overhead camshaft, five-speed machine. The much larger state-run factory at Stakonice absorbed Walter Motorcycles in 1949, but Jaroslav was allowed to continue development of his racers under the CZ name. Restrictions on travel meant that appearances by the Walter-CZ racers in the west were limited mainly to the Austrian and Isle of Man TTs. Nevertheless, they gave a good account of themselves, usually finishing in the top half dozen when they did appear. In 1958, Sammy Miller was selected to become the first British rider for decades to ride a works Czechoslovakian racer, and he rewarded CZ with second place in the 350cc Austrian TT. Sammy also challenged for the lead in the Lightweight IOM TT, and other successes would doubtless have followed if he had not then given up racing to concentrate on his trials career.

Sammy on a 250cc CZ at the 1958 TT

1937 250cc DKW

Although always based at Zschopau in Germany, DKW was actually founded by a Dane. Jorgen Rasmussen made domestic appliances until 1916, and then developed the Dampf Kraft Wagen (steam car) that gave his company its initials. After the Great War, Rasmussen began making a toy internal combustion engine that soon led to motorised cycles, and by 1926 DKW was mass-producing an extremely successful range of motorcycles. Racing was supported almost from the start, but the real breakthrough came in the 1930s with the 250cc and 350cc supercharged split single two-strokes developed by works engineers Weber and Prussing. Superficially, the engine looked like a V-twin, but whereas the upright cylinder housed the combustion chamber, the laid-down cylinder at the front was used to augment and compress the incoming petrol/air mixture. The result was unbeatable power, and an incredible exhaust note that could allegedly be heard eight miles away. In 1938, Ewald Kluge - riding a 250cc DKW like the one in the Museum - became the first German ever to win an IOM TT. That was almost the end of these unique machines, though, as supercharging was banned in post-War international competition, forcing DKW to develop totally new two-strokes.

1951
350cc Douglas 90 Plus

From its earliest days, the Douglas Company – situated at Bristol – was associated with horizontally opposed flat twin engines. Before WWII, the cylinders were almost invariably aligned with the frame, but afterwards a completely new model – the T35 – was launched with its engine set crosswise, in the BMW style. The T35 also had a revolutionary frame with Radiadraulic leading link forks, and torsion bar rear suspension, which gave excellent handling and comfort. Unfortunately, the model was under-developed, and Freddy Dixon - a legendary Douglas rider - was engaged as a consultant to deal with the many teething troubles. By 1950, he had helped to evolve the generally satisfactory Mark IV, and together with specialist dealer Eddy Withers, also developed Plus 80 and Plus 90 sports versions, whose model numbers indicated their maximum speeds. The latter variant, with its impressive nine-inch twin leading shoe front brake, was briefly the amateur's machine of choice in events like the Clubman's TT, until ousted by the simpler BSA Gold Star. Dixon personally prepared a few factory racers – one of which you see in the Museum – with further improvements that led to a top speed of 108mph being recorded in the Isle of Man.

DUNLOP TYRES
9

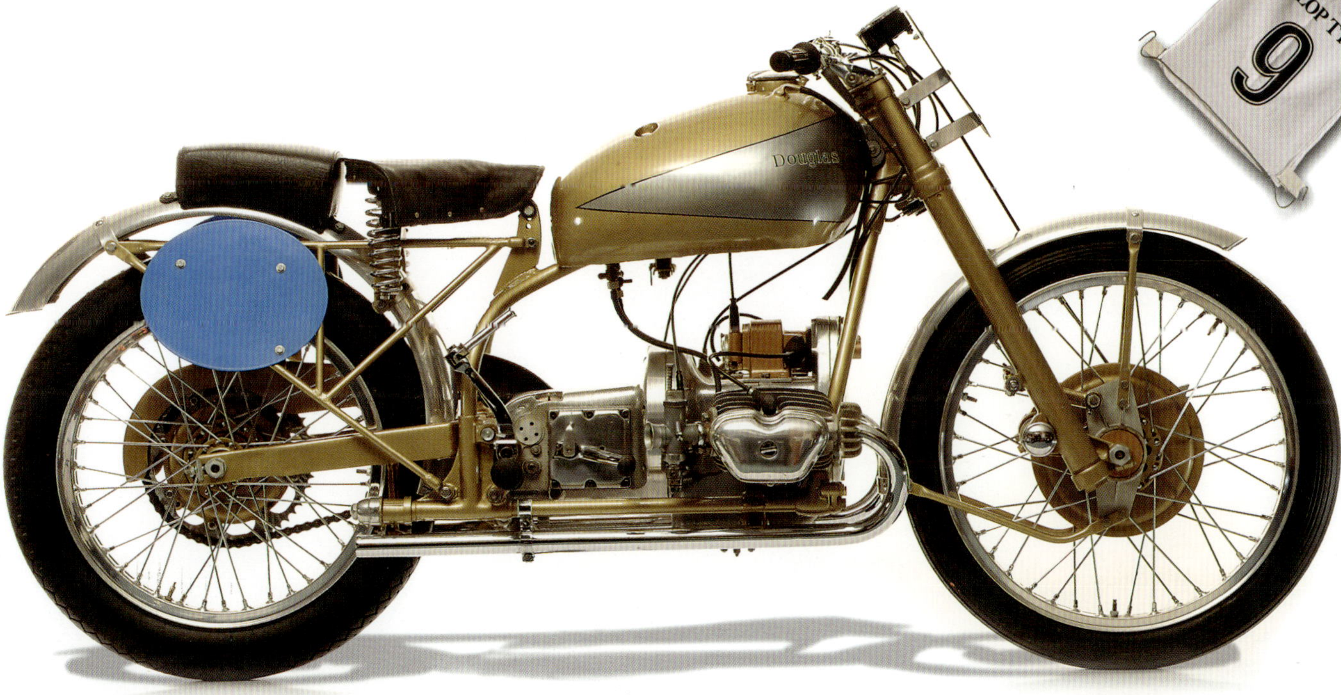
Douglas

1966
250cc DMW Hornet

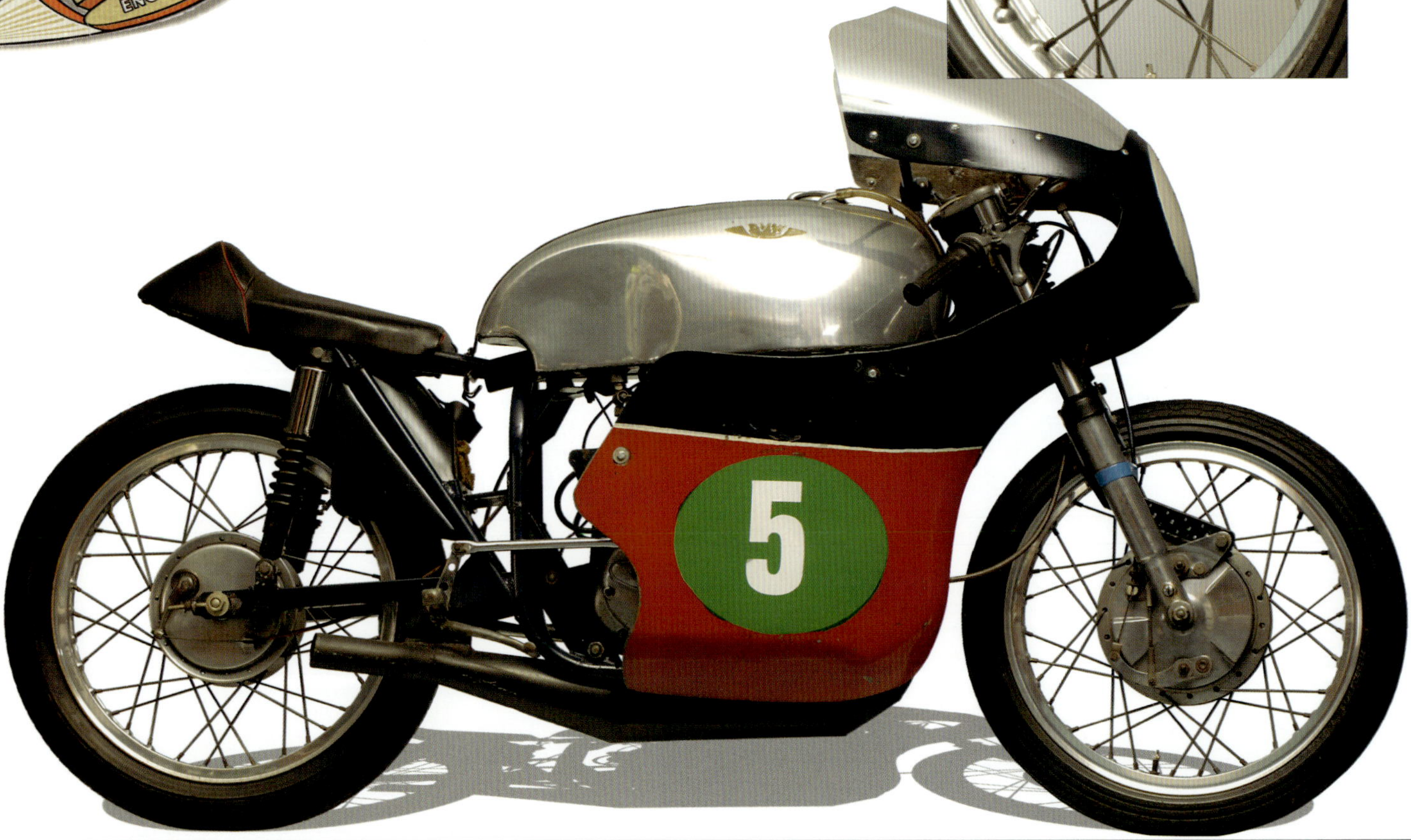

In the late-1940s, grasstrack racer 'Smoky' Dawson set up Dawson's Motorcycle Works in Wolverhampton. Naturally, its products included sporting variants, and in 1953 it was announced that an over-the-counter racer called the Hornet would shortly be put into production. This was to have a double overhead camshaft 125cc engine made by AMC (Ateliers de Mechanique du Centre – and no connection with the British concern bearing the same initials). Unfortunately production was delayed, and the project was abandoned with just a few racers manufactured, leaving DMW to concentrate on its successful roadsters, trials and scrambles machines. The advent of the Villiers Starmaker engine in the mid-1960s enabled the company - now run by Harold Nock - to revive its road racing aspirations, and the result, as seen in the Museum, also revived the model name. By now DMW controlled Metal Profiles Ltd, whose brakes and telescopic forks were naturally specified for its basic but purposeful production racer. The factory's own Hornet was raced with some success by Bill Smith - who also tested a 500cc prototype powered by twinned Starmaker engines - but DMW's racing involvement had ceased by time Harold Nock retired in 1972.

1948 350cc EMC

Austrian Dr Josef Ehrlich was greatly impressed by the two-strokes made during the 1930s by manufacturers in both his home country and Germany. These were 'split-singles' where a pair of pistons arranged in tandem operated off a common crankshaft; their different rates of rise and fall permitting better control of induction and exhaust than found in conventional single cylinder engines. After WWII the Doctor set up the Ehrlich Motor Company in London, where he made about 1500 350cc split-single roadsters over a six-year period. These machines failed to match his claims, as they had a modest power output, and their petrol consumption rose dramatically if wide throttle openings were used. Undaunted, he also developed a racing version, and the Museum's example shows many improvements - such as water-cooling and swinging arm rear suspension – compared with the roadster. This machine did produce acceptable power, but unfortunately, it had an even greater thirst, and one embarrassingly ran out of petrol in the 1947 Manx Grand Prix. Les Archer Jnr – who campaigned the actual machine seen in the Museum – had more success on mainland tracks, and rode a 250cc version to victory in the first Post-War Hutchinson 100 race meeting.

1952 125cc EMC

When Dr Josef Erhlich left Austria for England before the War, he brought with him two racing Puchs. Johann Puch had founded his business at Graz to make bicycles in 1891, and subsequently branched out into motorcycles. He died in 1914, but the company became part of the powerful Steyr-Daimler-Puch consortium and continued to make motorcycles, almost all of which had split-single two-stroke engines. These featured two pistons connected to a single crankshaft, and since one piston controlled the induction and the other managed the exhaust, the engine was significantly more efficient than a contemporary two-stroke with conventional porting. After the war Dr Ehrlich produced his own design of split-single 350cc motorcycles, but also continued his collaboration with Puch, who supplied him with 125cc racing engines to fit into machines like the one in the Museum. The engine's castings give dual credit to EMC and Puch, so Dr Joe probably carried out further development contributing to their many successes. EMC-Puchs gained top ten finishes in more than one 125cc TT, and Sammy Miller and John Surtees were just two of the notable riders who used these impressive machines before Ehrlich's racing efforts were put on hold in the mid-1950s.

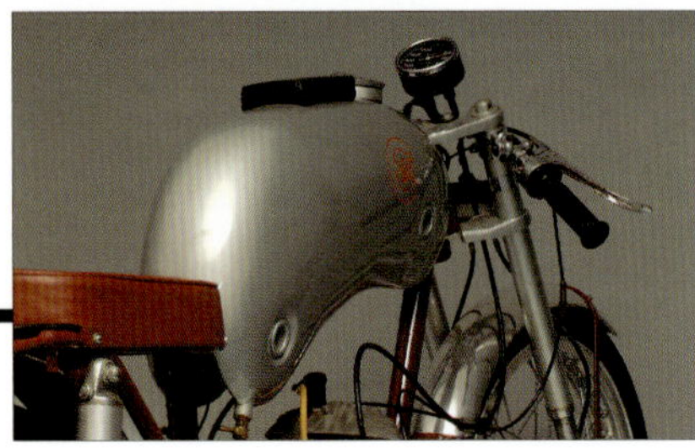

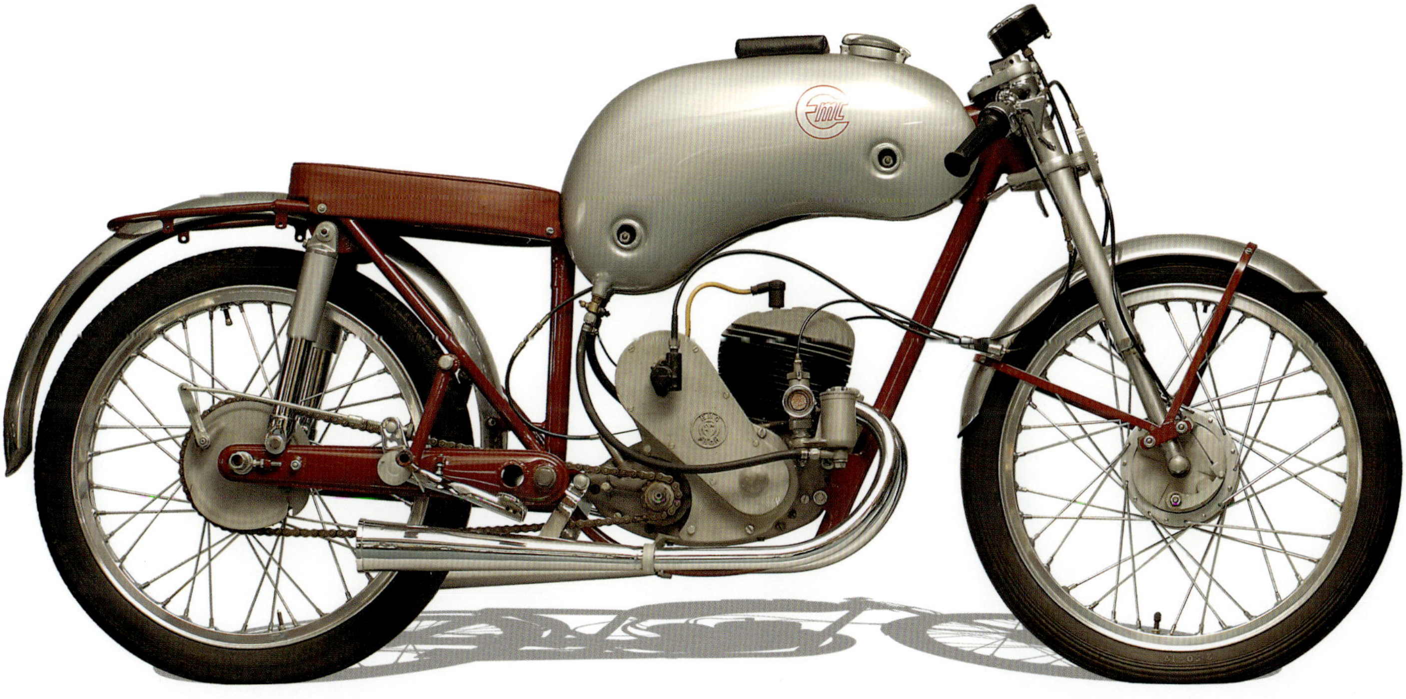
EMC

1931
1000cc Excelsior-JAP Silver Comet

Between the wars there was tremendous public interest in speed record attempts, and never more so than when BMW-mounted Ernst Henne and Englishman Joe Wright alternately held the record during 1930. At the end of the year, Wright was narrowly ahead on a Zenith that was controversially re-badged as an OEC, and his sponsor - Claude Temple – then unveiled a dramatic new machine designed to put the record beyond the German's reach. The engine was again a one litre vee-twin JAP, but it was boosted by a Powerplus supercharger, and gave no less than 100bhp at 5400rpm when running on methanol. This time the frame was made by Excelsior, and the machine was fully streamlined with polished steel fairings that earned it the nickname of Silver Comet. Wright recorded a record one-way speed of 163mph at Tat in Hungary, but the necessary return run was foiled by mechanical problems and bad weather. The Excelsior-JAP then fell into obscurity, until Sammy Miller discovered its engine in the mid-1980s. He then managed to source appropriate components to make a close reproduction of this extraordinary machine, whose side fairings and tail cone have been omitted in order to reveal the mechanical details.

"Excelsior"

1935
250cc Excelsior Manxman

Excelsior's best-known racer was undoubtedly the aptly nicknamed 'Mechanical Marvel', which won the 1933 Lightweight TT. However, its four-valve pushrod engine was both expensive to make and difficult to keep in tune, so it was soon abandoned in favour of a more conventional overhead camshaft design. The new model was named the Manxman, and – although it never won a TT - it proved to be a fast and reliable mount and its achievements included Stanley Woods' second place in the 1937 Lightweight event at an average speed of nearly 75mph. The Manxman had shaft and bevel gear drive to its two valves (a four valve, twin-carburettor prototype was found to be less reliable and no faster) and its advanced features included an optional bronze cylinder head with downdraught carburettor, and an alloy-finned barrel. The model was first listed in 1935, when it could be supplied for road and track use, and it was initially available in 250cc and 350cc forms, with a 500cc version being added to the range in 1936. The Museum's example was made in the first year of production.

1957 500cc Gilera

Gilera's world-renowned four-cylinder racers of the 1950s actually stemmed from one designed thirty years earlier by Carlo Gianni and Piero Remor. That machine was known as the Rondine, and by the mid-1930s it produced unbeatable power from its supercharged half-litre engine. Meanwhile Giuseppe Gilera had built up a thriving motorcycle business in a new factory at Arcore, and wanted to crown his achievements with machines that could excel in international racing. The opportunity arose when the Rondine's financial backer, Count Bonmartini, sold up, and the project continued under the Gilera name. After the war, Ing Remor redesigned the four in accordance with the ban on superchargers, and it was almost immediately successful with Masetti becoming World Champion in 1950. His main challenger was Norton's Geoff Duke, and when the Englishman joined the Gilera team in 1953 he became Champion three years in succession, besides helping to develop the machine to the specification seen in the Museum's example. The factory withdrew from GP racing for financial reasons in 1958 – shortly after Bob McIntyre's Gilera had achieved the first 100mph lap of the TT course - but Sammy has raced the Museum's superb replica in classic events throughout Europe and in New Zealand.

Goodwood Revival, 2006

5

1966
250cc Greeves RDS Silverstone

Greeves was one the more successful post-War British companies, and its products generally reflected founder Bert Greeves' own interest in off-road sport. Like most small manufacturers Greeves initially relied on Villiers engines, but rather than use them as supplied, the Essex-based concern carried out further development, and by the early 1960s their scrambler featured a square barrel top end with improved porting with a significantly greater power output. In 1962 the factory helped privateer Reg Everett to make a racer using mainly scrambler components – including Greeves' trademark leading link forks and alloy beam frame - and this was so successful that the next year the company introduced an over-the-counter version designated the 24 RAS Silverstone. During the next few years the Silverstone was progressively developed and by the time the Museum's RDS model was produced it featured Greeves' own engine producing over 35bhp, and had two Lightweight Manx GP wins and numerous short circuit successes to its credit. It had virtually reached its peak, however, and although a final RES version was launched the following year, it could not compete with technically more advanced racers coming from Bultaco and Yamaha, so production ceased in 1968.

1912 Humber

Humber was a pioneer company that moved from Nottinghamshire to Coventry, and by 1910 it was producing its own design of 198cc motorcycle. This set world speed records at Brooklands, and its success inspired Humber to introduce a radical new vee-twin model that could be supplied in various sports/touring guises. Its diminutive build resulted in a weight of less than 60kg (125lb), and its engine was technically very advanced with 'desaxe' cylinders to improve torque and reduce wear, and a novel in-line big end that maintained strength while minimising weight and friction. Most of all – in an era when a torquey long-stroke engine was usually considered essential – it had 'square' bore and stroke dimensions to boost engine revs and power. Many suspected that the new Humber would prove too fragile for long races, but six factory machines were entered in the 1911 TT, and all finished, with results including first and third places. Humber failed to follow up its success, however, only producing tourers after the Great War. The Museum's sparkling example of the little vee-twin is displayed in racing format to reflect its hour of glory, and Sammy paraded it in the Centenary re-enactment of the TT in 2007.

HUMBER
SHELL
LUBRICATING OIL

1962
125cc CR93 Honda

In its early days, Honda specialised in small capacity machines, and their CB92 roadster was quite competitive in the 125cc racing class, especially if fitted with the factory-supplied tuning kit. The firm soon saw a market opportunity, and early in 1962 introduced an over-the-counter production racer designated the CR93. Its twin cylinder motor was of advanced design with double overhead camshafts, 'square' bore and stroke dimensions and four valves per cylinder. Surprisingly, the Honda CR93 could be supplied in street-legal form with silencers and lights, but it's doubtful if any of these were sold in Britain, where they would have cost more than a home-produced big twin. For track use, however, the cost of over £600 was worthwhile, as the racing CR93's motor would produce 20bhp at 11,500rpm and it had a top speed of over 100mph when fitted with a fairing. In the hands of well-known racers like Bill Ivy and Rod Scivyer – who used one to win the 1966 British Championship – it immediately became the top machine in its class. Only 42 were imported to the UK during the two seasons that it was available and the Museum's CR93 is an exceptional survivor.

1963

250cc RC163 Honda

The first four cylinder Honda RC160 and RC161 racers were essentially doubled-up versions of the existing 125cc twins, with which they shared features such as shaft and bevel drive to the overhead camshafts. They made an impressive debut by taking five of the first six places in a Japanese event in August 1959, but they lacked world-class performance, so Honda set about a complete re-design. This resulted in the RC162, which set the pattern for future fours, and broke with previous practice in having chain camshaft drive. Up-and-coming rider Mike Hailwood became a works-supported private entrant in 1961, and in only his third ride on a Honda Four, proved its effectiveness and his own brilliance (he also won the 125cc and 500cc races) by achieving victory in the Lightweight Isle of Man TT. The Honda 250cc racer – with its innovations like four valves per cylinder – was now so successful that only minor revisions were needed to produce the following year's RC163 as seen in the Museum. On an RC163 Jim Redman took victory in both the 1962 and 1963 World Championships, and enlarged versions would soon spearhead Honda's assault on the larger classes.

SAMMY MILLER
HONDA
HONDA
2

1963
50cc CR110 Honda

On the 50cc Grand Prix circuit, Honda's RC111 works' racers usually had to play second fiddle to two strokes from Kreidler and Suzuki. That didn't stop the Hamamatsu-based company from concentrating on four-strokes, however, and in late 1961 Honda introduced the CR110 production racer, which had a top speed of well over 80mph and an engine that produced an impressive 8.5bhp. This wasn't achieved without high costs and technical complication, and the £330 racer had twin gear-driven overhead camshafts, four tiny valves per cylinder, and an eight-speed gearbox. With a carburettor size that would normally be seen on a half-litre roadster, and a very high compression ratio, the motor only ran properly above 8,000rpm and was not easy to use to its full potential as its power-band only began at 11,000rpm, while its life was drastically reduced if it was revved beyond 13,500rpm. Despite this, the CR110 was the machine of choice for top riders like Bill Ivy, Dave Simmonds and Chris Walpole, who came second on one in the 1963 50cc TT. The CR110 is now ultra-rare, as only 21 were imported to Britain before production stopped after just two seasons.

HONDA
50
CR110

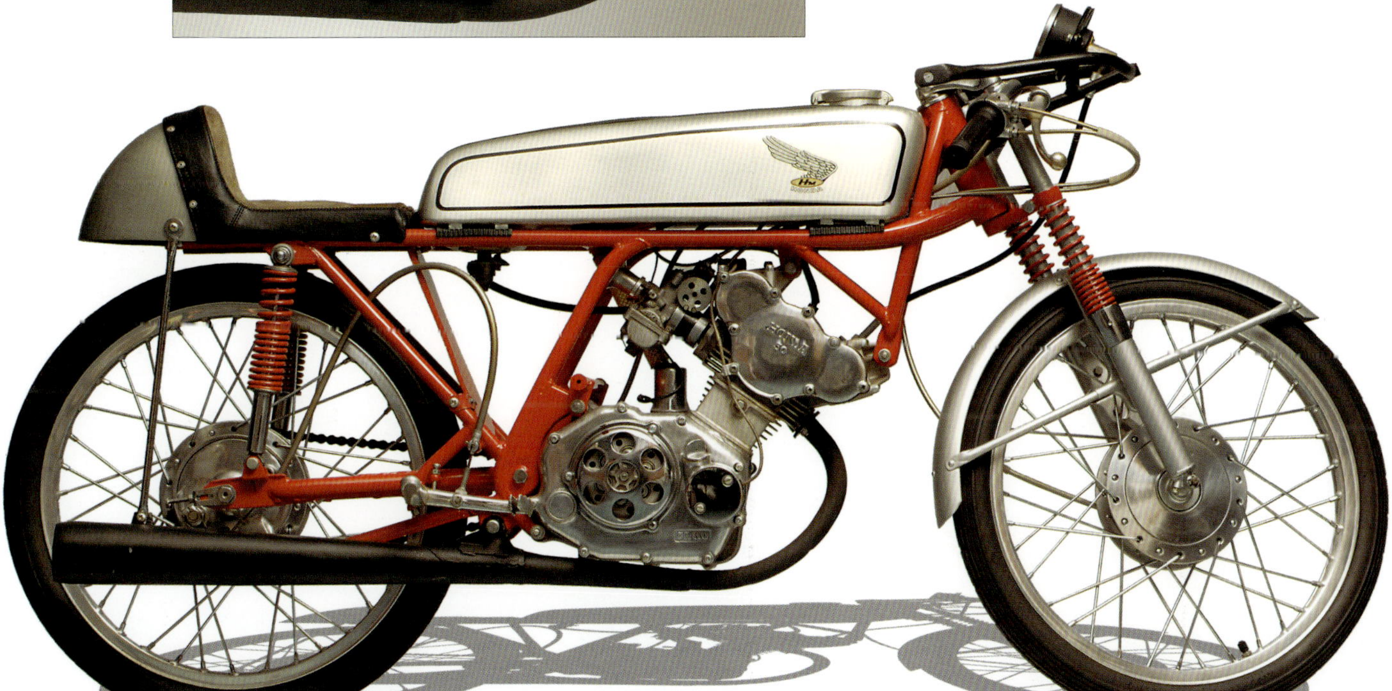

1935
500cc Husqvarna

Although best known in more recent years for its two-stroke scramblers, Husqvarna (named after its slightly differently spelt hometown of Huskvarna in Sweden) began life as an offshoot of an 18th century munitions concern. The firm then diversified into pedal cycles, and by 1903 had progressed to making complete motorcycles that it vigorously promoted through competition. Proprietary engines were used at this stage, but in 1926 Husqvarna began manufacturing its own V-twin engines. These were quite successful but uneconomic, and so a temporary return was made to JAP and Sturmey Archer engines. In about 1930, through experience gained with JAP engines Husqvarna produce a new 500cc in-house motor, and – while other manufacturers concentrated on single cylinder ohc racers - it was a pushrod operated ohv vee-twin. This distinctive motor was eventually developed to give 44bhp at 6800rpm, which gave a top speed of 120mph, and enabled its Swedish riders to win their own GP for three consecutive years from 1932. When Husqvarna's star rider tragically died in an accident, Norton rider Stanley Woods was recruited, and in 1935 – the year the Museum's rare example was made – he gave Husqvarna its fourth successive home victory.

HUSQVARNA

SAMMY MILLER MUSEUM
NEW MILTON
HAMPSHIRE
1935 HUSQUARNA 500cc
V-TWIN BORE 64.5mm STROKE 75mm
44 BHP @ 6,800 RPM
STANLEY WOODS RACED THIS TYPE
FOR HUSQUARNA FACTORY
HUSQVARNA
4

1967 340cc Jawa

In 1929 Czech Frantisek Janacek acquired the manufacturing rights to the German Wanderer motorcycle, and combined the companies' names to coin the word Jawa. In 1949 Jawa was nationalised by the communist government (along with CZ - its major rival) but was permitted to continue developing and racing the exotic double overhead camshaft twins and fours that were campaigned with distinction by stars like Franta Stasny. However, by the mid-1960s, Jawa had to accept that four-strokes were becoming outpaced in competition, and began experimenting with vee-twin two-stroke racers that did not prove particularly successful. The company's scramblers, on the other hand, were proving very competitive, despite being somewhat overshadowed by CZs. Just like Greeves in this country, Jawa saw that with relatively little development the motorcrosser's powerful engine and sturdy frame could be made into competent production racers, and the first was launched late in 1966. This featured a 250cc engine, which gave a respectable output of 31bhp at 7250rpm, and used the scrambler's unusual curved beam 'Flying Banana' chassis. The Museum's rare prototype, made the following year with the larger of Jawa's current motocross engines, was demonstrated by Graham Head at the 1996 TT Parade.

1980
KR500 Kawasaki

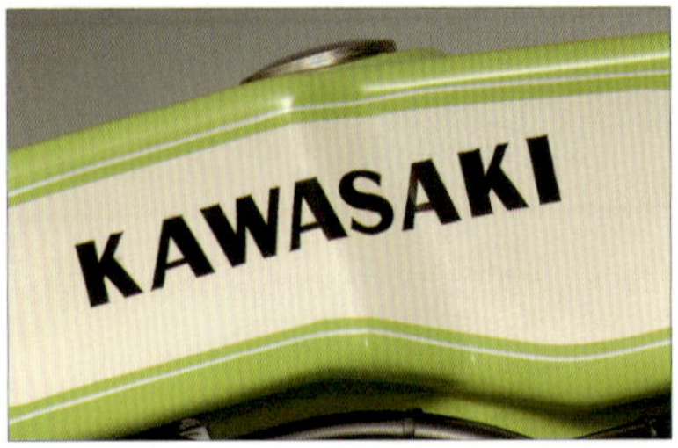

1969
500cc H1R Kawasaki

Kawasaki's two-stroke sports roadsters were extremely powerful, and by the mid 1960s were also being sold in tuned form for racing. The pattern continued with the arrival of the 500cc three-cylinder two-stroke H1 Mach III in 1968. Even in road trim this machine showed stunning performance and stamina in events like the 24hour Bol d'Or at Le Mans, and Kawasaki responded with the 1969 H1-R racing version. This had numerous detail improvements including a front disc brake and close ratio gears, and while the engine was still relatively conventional, with piston-controlled induction, it turned out a massive 72bhp at 9000rpm, giving a top speed of about 140mph. It experienced instant success in the Daytona 100 mile race, and in Europe, Ginger Molloy was only beaten in the Grand Prix series by Agostini's MV. The H1-R's only real weaknesses were an astonishing thirst for fuel and suspect handling inherited from Mach III, but it continued to achieve notable results like Mick Grant's second place in the 1973 Senior TT. That was effectively the end of the version seen in the Museum, however, as later models were updated with features like water-cooling, triple disc brakes and an improved frame.

KAWASAKI

1980
KR500 Kawasaki

Kawasaki's initial competition successes came in domestic motocross, soon after the company's first machines appeared in the early 1960s. Realising that Grand Prix racing success was essential for international fame, Kawasaki then unveiled a twin cylinder disc-valve 125cc two-stroke racer that, by 1969, had been developed into the firm's first World Championship winner. From the mid-1970s, Kawasaki came into GP racing in a big way, especially when South African Kork Ballington joined the team in 1978, and immediately won the next two years' 250cc and 350cc World titles on two-stroke twins. Predictably encouraged, in 1980 Kawasaki provided Ballington with the new KR500 racer, an inclined, liquid-cooled, disc-valve square four that was effectively a doubling up of the successful 250cc twin. As can be seen in the Museum's exhibit – allocated to Ballington, but never raced – the machine's chassis was as revolutionary as its magnesium-cased engine, its aluminium monocoque construction helping to reduce weight below 140kgs, note the anti-dive front suspension. Unfortunately, the KR500 never lived up to expectations - its best result being Ballington's 1982 British National title - and it proved to be the firm's GP swansong with Kawasaki retiring from top-class racing at the end of that year.

1969 500cc Linto

Linto is a contraction of Lino Tonti, the name of the machine's maker. Tonti had been Aermacchi's designer before departing for Mondial and Bianchi in the mid-1950s, and his successor, Alfredo Bianchi (no relation) then designed the single-cylinder roadster that was developed into the successful 250cc Ala d'Oro production racer. Aermacchi made various attempts to enlarge this into a viable competitor in the 500cc class, but none had been overly successful by the time Tonti re-entered the story in 1968. Working privately (despite being employed by Moto Guzzi) he took the cylinders and heads from two Ala d'Oro short-stroke engines, and mounted them on a specially made bottom end. The cylinders were laid down Aermacchi-style, and there was gear primary drive to the six-speed gearbox. After a year's development, during which Alberto Pagani won the Imola GP, one batch of fifteen Lintos was made. Two were retained for 'works' riders Pagani and Jack Findlay, while the others were sold to leading privateers. The machines had a creditable 64bhp at 10,000rpm, moderate weight and excellent handling, but unfortunately all this was cancelled out by poor reliability, and the Imola victory remained the only highlight of the Linto's short career.

linto

1954 Matchless G45

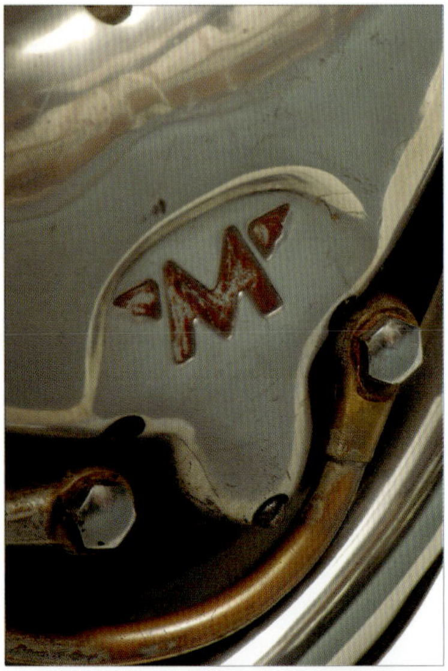

Despite its founders' personal interests – Charles and Harry Collier achieving several wins and places in early TTs – Matchless did not have any serious racing involvement between the World Wars. However, the post-War introduction of Clubman's TT races, plus the launch of the sporty new 500cc Matchless G9 twin, encouraged the London-based firm to try again. The result appeared in 1950 as the Model G45, and it closely followed the G9's design, with a three bearing crankshaft and pushrod valve operation. In fact the differences were only in the detail; the iron crankshaft, for instance, being replaced by a one-piece steel item with shrunk-on flywheels. The machine made an encouraging start, with Robin Sherry riding the prototype to fourth place in the 1951 Senior Manx GP, and Derek Farrant taking first place the following year. Matchless then made the G45 available to private buyers, fitting the tuned engine into the established AJS 7R frame, but the engine suffered from a narrow power band, and the extent to which it could be further developed was limited by the pushrod valve operation. In 1958 the G45 was replaced by the ohc G50 with just the one major victory to its name.

1934
250cc Excelsior Mechanical Marvel

Employing four valves per cylinder is an obvious way of increasing exhaust and inlet areas, and in 1933 Excelsior fully exploited the principle with two downdraught carburettors feeding individual inlet ports, and separate exhausts. A hemispherical combustion chamber was considered essential for maximum efficiency, so the valves were inevitably oriented in four different directions, which considerably complicated Ike Hatch's design. Separate inlet and exhaust camshafts in the crankcase operated cam followers, splayed pushrods then moved small pistons in the cylinder head, and these drove the valves via rockers supported on roller bearings. The rockers were greased, the pushrods and cams used the main oil supply, and the valve guides had a separate feed of a different grade of oil. It's no wonder that the machine was christened the Mechanical Marvel, or that it was plagued by poor reliability after a sensational debut when it won the 1933 Lightweight TT for Sid Gleave! Only four were made before it was replaced by the more conventional Manxman, and in 1995 Sammy Miller discovered this ultra-rare survivor in France where it had remained ever since factory teamster Ted Mellors rode it to third place in the 1934 French GP.

Excelsior

2
Excelsior

1953
125cc Reynolds-Mondial Special

By 1952, the World Championship winning dohc 125cc Mondial was becoming uncompetitive against its Italian competitors, and coincidentally, Englishman Maurice Cann was approaching the end of his career with Moto Guzzi. Observing that the duplex McCandless Featherbed frame made by tube specialists Reynolds had rejuvenated the outdated Manx Norton, Cann acquired a Mondial works engine, and commissioned a frame for it. The job was given to Reynolds employee Ken Sprayson, who - with no in-house design experience to guide him - used the Earles' leading link fork for which his employers currently had manufacturing rights, and made a frame based on the Featherbed. This had top frame tubes that crossed each other near the headstock creating stiffness and – importantly for a lightweight – making the whole motorcycle lower and more streamlined. The machine was successful enough for Sprayson to become the country's best-known fabricator of special frames, and also enabled Maurice Cann to prolong his career for several years. The Reynolds-Mondial then passed through other hands and was extensively modified before being discovered by Sammy Miller, and restored in 2006. Testing it on behalf of Classic MotorCycle magazine, the author found that it still has impressive power and superb handling.

3

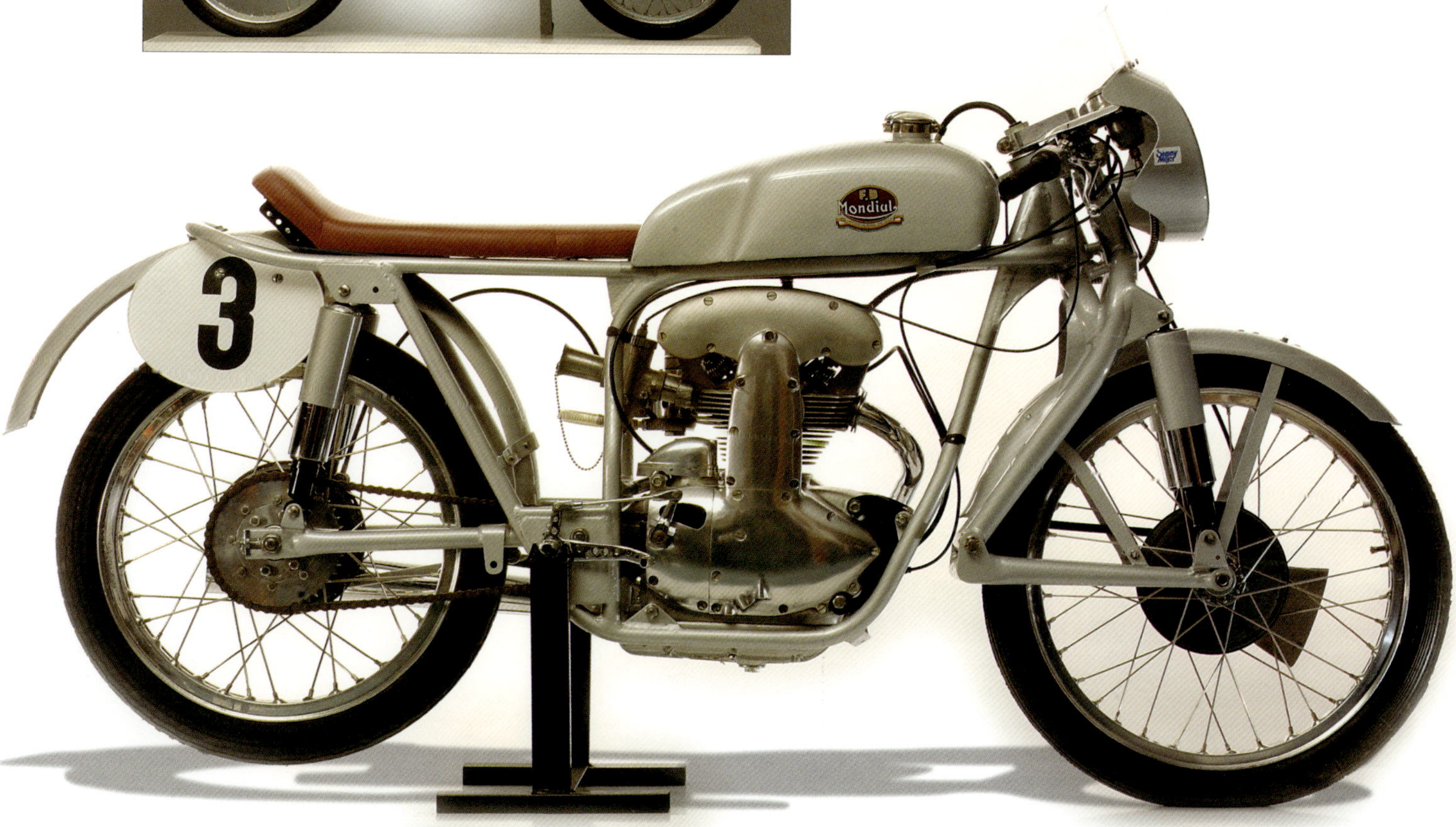
F.B
Mondial
3

1957
250cc DOHC Mondial

Mondial's earlier twin cylinder dohc quarter litre Grand Prix challenger had proved unsuccessful - largely because of its exceptionally narrow power band – and in 1957 the Bologna company unveiled a totally new 250cc single. With 29bhp at 10,800rpm, seven speed gearbox and full streamlining (shortly to be banned by the FIM because of riders' concerns about instability in windy conditions) its top speed was almost 140mph. A young Sammy Miller was recruited as works rider, along with the established Cecil Sandford, and he gave the new machine a spectacular debut. Only a seized gearbox on almost the last corner prevented Sammy from winning the Lightweight TT ahead of Sandford (he courageously pushed in to fifth place after crashing) and he finished the season third in the World Championship. Unfortunately, that was the end of a very promising partnership, as rising costs forced Mondial (together with Gilera and Moto Guzzi) to temporarily retire from Grand Prix racing, and Sammy decided to concentrate on his trials career. He still had the ex-Works racer, though, and managing to locate the Italian craftsman who had panel-beaten the original aluminium streamlining, he commisioned another set to complete the Museum's gleaming restoration.

Ulster GP, 1957

11
Sammy Miller
Mondial

1951

250cc Moto Guzzi Gambalunghino

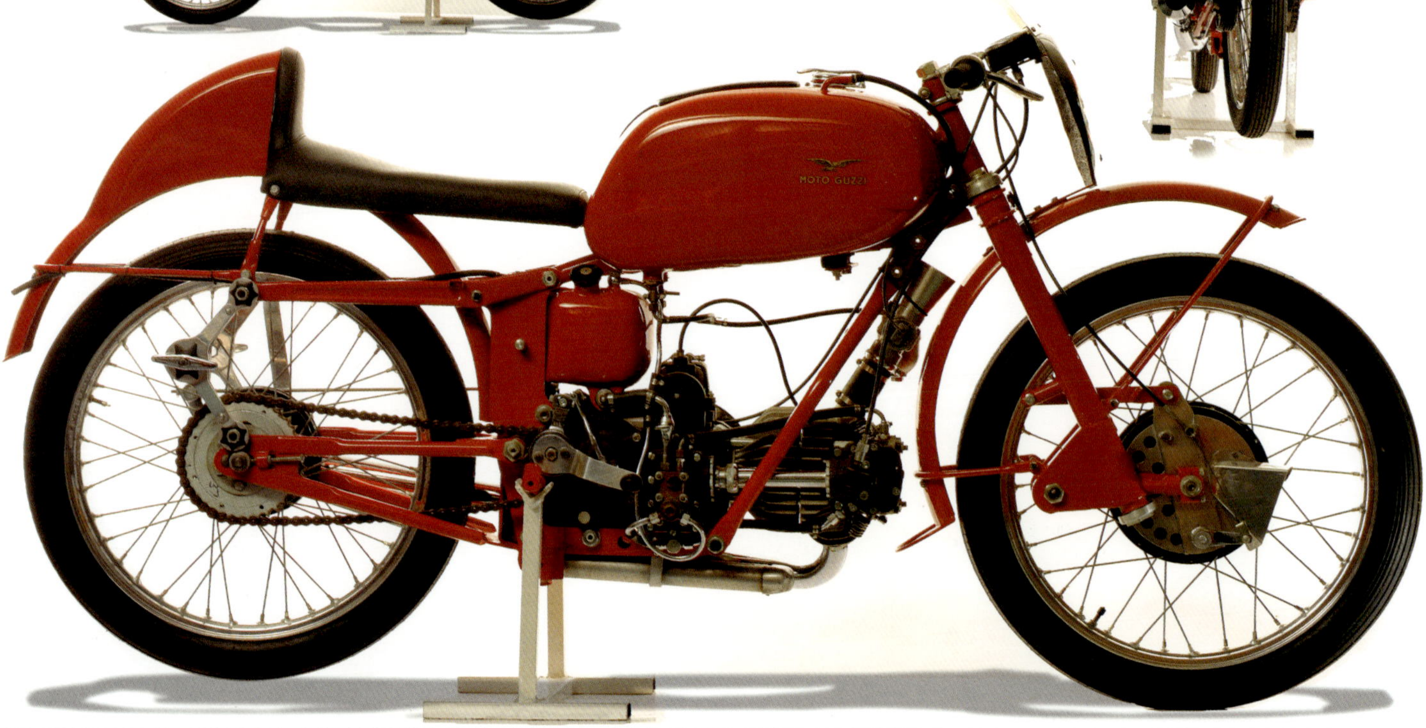

Until comparatively recent years (and despite experiments with twin, triple, four and eight cylinder racers) Moto Guzzi was mostly associated with laid-down single cylinder engines. The Mandello marque's more successful racers of the early post-war years were no exception, the best-known example being the 500cc Gambalunga – a nickname that means 'Long Leg' in Italian. So when Moto Guzzi developed the smaller but similar-looking Albatross into a more advanced 250cc single overhead camshaft racer in 1949, it was predictably christened the Gambalunghino, or 'Little Long Leg'. It was instantly successful; its 28bhp engine and top speed of over 100mph being sufficient for it to win three of the four races that made up that year's World Championship. Strangely enough, the three works riders – Manliff Barrington, Maurice Cann and Bruno Ruffo – each won one race, and the latter was eventually named Champion on account of his better second-place record. With its outside flywheel and friction damping on the rear suspension, the Gambalunghino – like many other Moto Guzzis - looks archaic and unorthodox to British eyes, but developments of it were effective enough to win further 250cc World Championships, and to be stretched into challengers for the larger classes.

c1950
500cc Moto Guzzi Dondolino

The first 500cc Moto Guzzi production racer was the GTC of 1937, which was quickly supplemented by the more ambitious Condor, with its close-ratio gears and aluminium cylinder head and barrel. Crucially, its weight was minimal - with aircraft-grade aluminium alloy used in the frame - and the laid-down engine gave a minimal frontal area, so the Condor's modest horsepower provided enough speed to win the important Lario road race. After WWII, Moto Guzzi quickly updated the design into the Dondolino, and its enhanced power immediately led to victory in the 1946 Swiss Grand Prix. Dondolino means 'Rocking Chair' in Italian, and presumably alluded to the comfort given by the machine's sophisticated swinging fork rear suspension, although critics joked that it referred to cornering instability at speed. Contemporary factory riders were soon supplied with the more highly developed long-stroke Gambalunga, but that came and went in a couple of years, while the over-the-counter Dondolino continued to be available to the private enthusiasts into the mid-1950s, and was still effective enough to win several prestigious Milan-Taranto road races. The machine was evidently equally popular abroad, as the Museum's Dondolino was discovered in Argentina in a complete but very poor condition.

MOTO GUZZI

1953
125cc MV Agusta

Mention of MV Agusta inevitably brings to mind the exotic multi-cylinder 'fire engines' of the 1960s, but Count Domenico Agusta's aeronautical company only turned to motorcycles after WWII, and its first product was a modest 98cc two-stroke. This was soon being tuned and raced, and in 1948 a 125cc version became available as a production racer. Although adequate for National races it was out-classed by the four-stroke Mondial in World Championships, so Count Agusta lured top designers Magni and Remor away from Gilera, and they designed double overhead camshaft 125cc singles and 500cc fours that shared cylinder dimensions and mechanical details. The smaller model almost immediately gave Cecil Sandford the 1952 World Championship, and again MV Agusta responded to customer demand by putting a 125cc production racer on sale. Somewhat tamer than the works bikes, this had a single overhead camshaft, and came with street legal equipment, since lights and a kickstart were required for road-based events like the Giro d'Italia. Once these items were abandoned, however, the Sport Competizione was an extremely effective machine on the track, and the Museum's little MV was used in the 1953 Ultra-Lightweight TT, when Arnold Jones rode it to fifth place.

c1972
750cc MV Agusta

Count Domenico Agusta was the inspiration behind the fabulous Gallarate triples and fours that won so many championships. When he died of a heart attack in 1971 the effort inevitably slackened - despite a last 500cc championship with Phil Read in 1974 - and the team was officially wound up in 1976. But that wasn't the whole story, as for many years MV had (rather reluctantly) also made road-going versions of its fours. Private owners had always been discouraged from racing these roadsters, and that was allegedly part of the reason they were given shaft-drive, although in fairness it should be noted that the very first factory racers were also shaft-driven. However, the reduction in the Grand Prix effort persuaded the factory to try what it had advised owners not to do, and some 750cc dohc fours were prepared as racers, one of which Giacomo Agostini rode at Imola in 1972. These machines were often subsequently converted to chain rear drive, and the Museum's example was raced at both Imola and Daytona under the Team Firenze banner. Since acquiring it, Sammy Miller has delighted MV's countless fans by enthusiastically demonstrating the MV at Goodwood, the Isle of Man and elsewhere.

1934
250cc New Imperial

This almost forgotten marque is close to Sammy Miller's heart, for he won his very first race – the 1953 Temple grass track in Northern Ireland – on a 150cc New Imperial. The firm had a patchy record in sport, setting Brooklands records in the early 1920s with an experimental overhead camshaft engine that JAP subsequently declined to put into production, and veering between success and failure in the TT. New Imperial continued to innovate, however, manufacturing its own engines after 1926, and pioneering the use of pivoted fork rear suspension and unit construction engines in the early-1930s. Interestingly, the 250cc and 350cc GP racers announced in 1934 were relatively conventional, with a full-loop rigid frame and a separate four-speed gearbox. They were available to the wealthy clubman, but the museum's racer is an ex-works 250cc model of the type supplied to factory riders like Charlie Dodson. The model's achievements were limited because the Birmingham concern's racing effort was currently dissipated on an unsuccessful 500cc vee-twin, but in 1936 Bob Foster won the Lightweight TT on a unit-construction New Imperial. Unfortunately, it was too late for the publicity to save the firm, and motorcycle production ceased soon afterwards.

NEW
IMPERIAL

55
NEW
IMPERIAL

1955/6
350cc Model F Norton

Doubtless influenced by Moto Guzzi's recent run of success with compact machines featuring laid-down single cylinder engines, in 1955 the Norton race-shop began work on the similarly configured Model F, the letter standing for 'Flat'. Although the engine was based on the current Manx, this was far from being a simple exercise. The engine – which had an external flywheel to reduce oil drag and crankcase size - had to be unitised with the gearbox to keep its length within bounds, but it still did not fit the Featherbed frame, so an oil-carrying spine replacement was designed. The engine/gearbox castings were in Elektron magnesium alloy to reduce weight, and there was spur gear primary drive to an innovative five-speed gearbox, which had a novel pinion arrangement to minimise its size. The engine gave as much power as the current upright engine, and - with a lower centre of gravity and smaller frontal area – the Model F's prospects looked extremely promising. Unfortunately, Bracebridge Street's management then decided that the race team ought to campaign standard-looking Manx racers, rather than works specials, so one of the most innovative Norton racers ever made was tragically hidden away and never raced.

1953
350cc Norton 'Silver Fish' Kneeler

The experimental Kneeler was the definitive attempt to improve the obsolescent Manx Norton's performance with better streamlining, and its rider laid virtually prone to minimise the frontal area. The top tubes of the Featherbed-based frame were splayed out around the engine, fuel was pumped up from pannier tanks beside the engine, and the full aluminium streamlining immediately gave the machine its alternative nickname of Silver Fish. As a schoolboy Sammy Miller heard rumours of this secret semi-works project - made in Belfast by Artie Bell, the McCandless brothers and the Short Aircraft Company - and he saw it make a promising debut in the 1953 North West 200 race, where works rider Ray Amm set a lap record before retiring with fuel pump problems. The Silver Fish was never seriously raced again, mainly because of qualms about the stability of streamlined machines in winds, but Ray Amm and Eric Oliver used it to set numerous speed records at Montlhéry. In 1984 Sammy paraded the newly restored Kneeler in the North West 200, and only his quick reactions prevented disaster when the fuel starvation problem that terminated Ray Amm's ride re-occurred while he was flat out on the straight.

Cylinder head from the experimental rotary-valve Norton

SMITHS
R.P.M.×10

Norton

1960
350cc Lowboy Norton

Lowboy reunited with fairing after 48 years

Like the Silver-Fish Kneeler of the early-1950s, the Lowboy was an attempt to compensate for a Manx Norton's limited power by reducing its frontal area. This time, race chief Doug Hele employed a virtually standard Featherbed frame, but fitted the petrol tank below the seat, and put the oil tank behind the gearbox, which necessitated minor alterations to the rear frame and swinging arm. With the rider's chin virtually resting on the cam-box, it was impossible to see past conventional forks, so the fork legs were shortened and welded directly to a massive bottom yoke. The steering head remains, however, and still seriously limits forward vision. The Lowboy's only rider when new was TT specialist Eddie Crooks, who secretly tried it out during the 1960 TT. He found that the lack of support from a fuel tank put so much strain on his wrists that he couldn't remain low enough to take advantage of the machine's build, and the Lowboy was retired after just one lap of the Isle of Man. Fortunately, it was saved from the scrap heap by Norton employee the late Bob Colller, and has recently been re-united with its original fairing.

1955
250cc Sportmax NSU

After NSU's twin cylinder dohc Rennmax works racers had dominated the quarter-litre GP class for several years, the 1954 news that there would be no works team using it in future World Championships came as a complete shock. In compensation, however, the German company announced that the road-going Max would be developed into a production racer called the Sportsmax. The Max had an innovative single overhead camshaft engine that already made it the fastest 250cc motorcycle on the road, so it wasn't surprising that it could be easily turned into the quickest available production racer. What was remarkable, however, was that the 28bhp/125mph Sportsmax immediately took over the Rennmax's mantle at International level, with veteran Hermann Muller winning the 1955 250cc World Championship. Only about twenty genuine Sportsmax machines were built (although many Max Roadsters were converted privately) and their riders over the next few years included many of the top riders of the day, including John Surtees, Mike Hailwood and Sammy Miller. Sammy's fantastic record on the Museum's fully-faired Sportsmax includes second places in the 1955 and 1956 Ulster GPs, three consecutive victories in the North-West 200, and more than 35 other wins in Irish road races.

North West 200, 1956

The IOM TT Past Masters' Parade, 1986

The German GP, Hanover, 1957

1957 250cc Parilla

After running a motor engineering business in Milan, Giovanni Parrilla began manufacturing complete motorcycles (spelling their name slightly differently) in 1946. Always interested in achieving high performance, his first road and race motorcycles had single overhead camshaft 250cc engines, and almost immediately work was started on an even more ambitious dohc version with Elektron alloy castings. This won the 1950 Milan-Taranto road race, and a 350cc version exported to Germany temporarily dominated sport there, even outperforming the DKW racers. Perhaps having overstretched himself, Parrilla then dropped out of top-flight racing in order to concentrate on the manufacture of road machines and production racers powered by a high-cam ohv engine. The first of these was the 175cc Competizione, which was renamed the MDS when telescopic forks replaced its Earles-type leading link forks, and it was soon joined by 200cc and 250cc versions. The 'Hi-Cam' racers as seen in the Museum were almost exclusively exported to America, where they proved especially successful, winning events well into the 1960s. The firm itself fell victim to a slump in sales, and ceased making motorcycles in 1967, but continued to use its racing expertise in the manufacture of successful go-kart engines.

MOTO
PARILLA

1937
250cc OK Supreme

OK motorcycles were made by Ernest Humphries and Frederick Dawes, and first appeared in 1899. The partners often disagreed over business matters, and Dawes departed in 1926, leaving Black Ernie – as he was nicknamed on account of his uncontrollable temper – to add Supreme to the business title, and to make exclusive and innovative motorcycles until the outbreak of WWII. Humphries now had a freer hand to go racing, and his JAP-powered machines gained several good TT results, highlighted by Frank Longman's win in 1928. Not wanting to rely on proprietary engines, Humphries then introduced the famous 'Lighthouse' model, with its trademark cylinder head window, through which the rider could observe the action of cams formed at the top of a vertical shaft. It was popular on the road, but not the hoped-for success on the track, and in 1934 it was replaced by the Silver Cloud, which had conventional shaft drive to an overhead camshaft running across the head. The Museum's machine is an ex-works racer based on the Silver Cloud and was ridden by post-War World Champion Les Graham, but, despite attracting such high-class riders, the later OK Supreme's best result was tenth place in the 1938 TT.

SUPREME

1966
250cc GP5 Royal Enfield

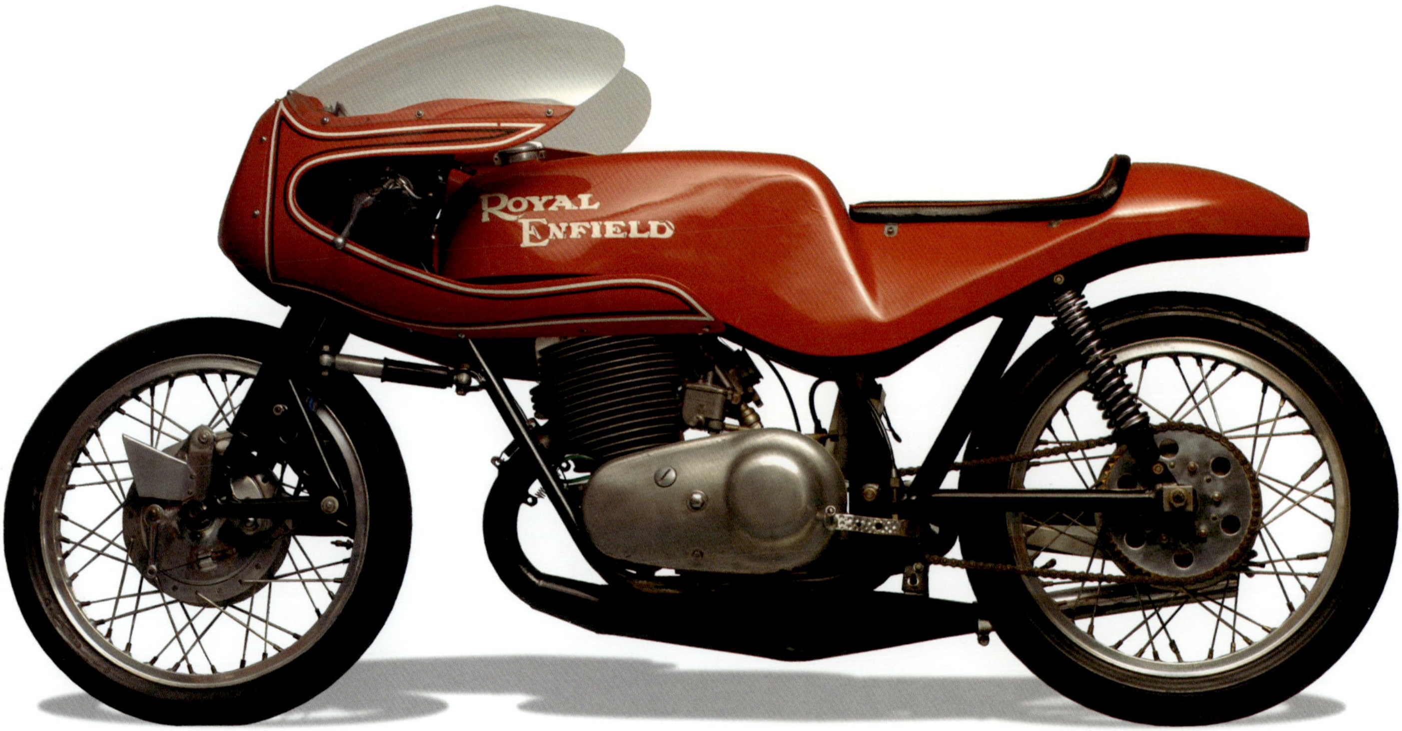

Most of Royal Enfield's sporting successes were in off-road events, so the 1964 announcement that the Redditch factory intended to make a 250cc production racer was a considerable surprise. As with several other manufacturers, the catalyst was the Villiers Starmaker competition engine, which could be bought and used without further tuning. Unlike the others, however, RE quickly decided to abandon the Villiers engine, and to develop its own power unit. The result was unveiled in early 1964 as the GP5, and featured an Alpha bottom end in heavily finned crankcases, an Amal GP carburettor, and a cylinder barrel with porting designed by two-stroke maestro Hermann Meier. A new duplex frame was topped off with a stylish glass fibre tank/seat unit, and an outing in the Manx GP was sufficiently encouraging for the company to build a batch of twenty or so replicas, and to engage ex-Norton and Gilera superstar Geoff Duke as manager of a works team. GP5 riders included John Hartle, Percy Tait and TT-specialist Neil Kelly, but when significant success eluded them, RE's involvement inevitably slackened (although Tait continued to ride Duke's privately-entered GP5) and was finally axed when Norton-Villiers absorbed the firm in 1967.

1926

350cc TT Model Rex Acme

The Rex motorcycle company was founded in 1899, and in 1921 amalgamated with the neighbouring Coventry Acme Company to make Rex-Acme motorcycles powered by proprietary motors. Well aware of the publicity to be gained from competition successes, the new firm immediately went racing, and was rewarded with numerous TT wins and places in the next few years, especially after engaging current superstar Walter (Wal) Handley. To cash in on these successes, Rex-Acme understandably and deservedly incorporated the Isle of Man's three-legged crest into their tank badge, and also produced Tourist Trophy Models (or TT replicas) like the one in the Museum. The author has reported on this machine for the Classic MotorCycle magazine, and was highly impressed by its top-notch ancillary parts that include Webb forks, a four-speed Burman gearbox, an Enfield cush-drive hub and a trigger operated steering damper. More importantly, its outside flywheel Blackburne engine gives it a top speed higher than that of many similarly sized machines made thirty years later. Even its riding position (and exhaust note!) would be familiar to a coffee bar cowboy from a later generation. Unfortunately, Rex-Acme became an early victim of the financial recession, and made no more motorcycles after 1930.

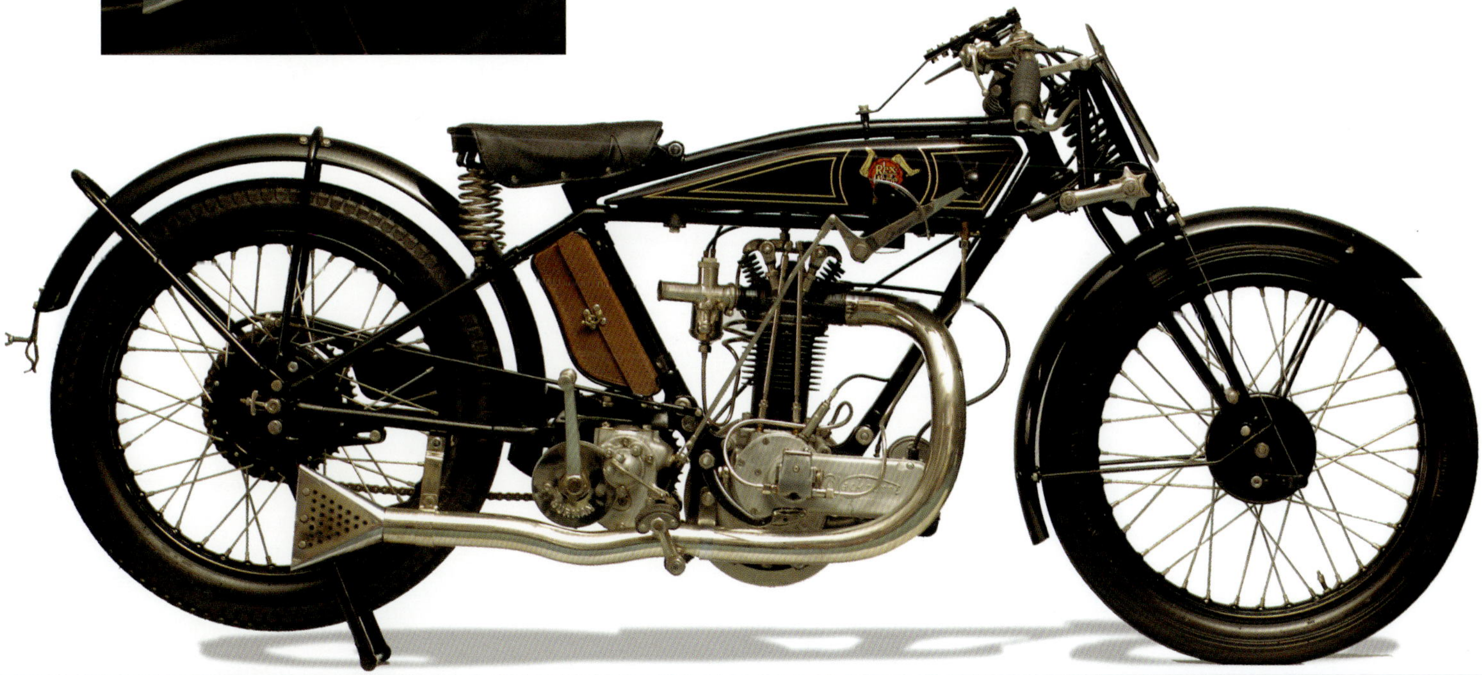

1934
250cc Radial Valve Rudge

While many firms were folding or retrenching at the start of the economic depression, Graham Walker's record 80mph-plus winning speed in the 1928 Ulster GP set Rudge on course for new heights of innovation and success. The single cylinder racing engine already featured four valves – to increase valve area and reduce the reciprocating mass – with the pairs of inlet and exhaust valves set parallel in a pent roof combustion chamber. In 1930, however, designer George Hack unveiled an ambitious new 350cc engine with a more efficiently shaped hemispherical combustion chamber. There were again four pushrod-operated valves, but now they were arranged radially, and actuated by a complex array of no less than six rockers. The machine was an instant success, with works riders Tyrell-Smith, Walker and Nott taking the first three places in the Junior TT. A 250cc version – like the one in the Museum - then joined the range, and was equally successful, winning the 1931 Lightweight TT for Graham Walker (father of television commentator Murray) among many other victories. In 1933, the economic situation forced Rudge to drop out of racing, but production of high quality road machines and proprietary engines continued until 1939.

Rudge

1967
500cc Pre-Spondon Phantom

In 1967, amateur racer Bob Stevenson was considering making a new frame for his BSA Gold Star, when his friend Geoff Galloway suggested something much more radical. The Phantom was the result, and it featured paired Greeves Silverstone engines in a homemade frame constructed from Reynolds steel tubing. Working in a garden shed and at technical college classes, Geoff and Bob also developed the linkage between the motors, leading link forks, and many other parts including the brakes. Stevenson himself raced the Phantom for a while, finding that the sudden power delivery taxed both his and the frame's capabilities, but becoming enthusiastic enough to leave his job with Rolls Royce and set up a motorcycle engineering business named after its Derbyshire hometown. Spondon frames are still being made, and they have featured on many notable motorcycles including Martin Wimmer's 1982 British Championship-winning Yamaha, and the rotary Nortons that won two successive F1 Championships in the 1990s. The Phantom, meanwhile was campaigned by Fred Huyer while it was being further developed and tamed with Concentric carburettors and Spondon telescopic forks. It then gathered dust at Spondon Engineering until Geoff Galloway kindly donated it for restoration and display at the Museum.

1933
500cc Sunbeam 95

Sunbeam maintained an unmatched reputation for quality and performance until they ceased making traditional motorcycles at the start of WWII. Never the most innovative of manufacturers, Sunbeam continued racing side valve machines until they were outdated in the mid-1920s, and quickly reverted to pushrod valve operation after a brief flirtation with overhead camshafts. However, the race team didn't lack success, and after team leader Graham Walker moved to Rudge, his shoes were ably filled by the likes of George Dance, Alec Bennett and Charlie Dodson (who won the Senior TT in 1928 and 1929). The works team was disbanded after 1930, but Sunbeams continued to be raced, as the works machines were essentially specially prepared roadsters, and in 1933 the sportier models could still be bought over the counter and used on the road, or prepared for the track. The Museum's Model 95 was ridden by Walter Rusk, and along with another great Irish rider, Artie Bell, he reportedly made test runs on it along the Antrim coastal road on Sunday mornings. Rusk's practice and preparation were rewarded by a record lap in the 1933 Senior TT, the fastest time ever recorded by a Sunbeam.

THE
95
SUNBEAM

THE
95
SUNBEAM

3

1980
500cc Suzuki RG500 Mk V

The Suzuki RG500 was one of the greatest racing motorcycles ever, and among its many achievements it allowed team leader Barry Sheen to win his two Senior World Championships, and gave multiple Senior TT victories to semi-works riders like Mick Grant and Graeme Crosby. Its engine was a disc-valve square-four two-stroke, a format that had been tried in 1963, when the championship-winning 125cc twin had been doubled up to challenge Honda for honours in the lightweight class. That machine had been a temperamental failure, but Suzuki had evidently learnt a lot before launching the 500cc Four ten years later, and its engine was powerful and reliable. It was initially somewhat intractable, and the handling was suspect, but two years of careful development meant that when ridden by Barry Sheen at the peak of his form in 1976/7, the RG500 was virtually unbeatable. A measure of its capability is that in 1976, other RG500s took the next five top positions in the championship as well. Yamaha then temporarily became ascendant, but development of the RG500 continued, and soon after the Museum's MkV RG500 had been made, works rider Marco Lucchinelli was able to bring the Championship back to Suzuki.

1929
350cc Velocette Mk I KTT

After initially making four-stroke motorcycles, Veloce Ltd produced a series of two-strokes called Velocette (or little Veloce) which were so well-regarded that the name was adopted for all their subsequent machines. Veloce gained respectable racing results with their two-strokes, but that was nothing compared with their achievements after re-entering the four-stroke scene in 1925. The new Model K – designed by Percy Goodman, the son of the firm's founder - had a single overhead camshaft engine, and its basic design was so sound that it was carried forward to all subsequent Velocette racers. The model could be purchased in various states of tune, but the pure racing version was naturally given the KTT designation in recognition of Junior TT wins by works-rider Alec Bennett in 1926 and 1928 (when he recorded the first 70mph-plus lap in this class). At Montlhéry that year, Harold Willis also raised the one-hour 350cc speed record to over 100mph, and the MkI KTT immediately became the clubman's machine of choice. Virtually everything about it was 'right', and by the time the Museum's model was made, that included the newly introduced positive-stop gear change, a feature so innovatory and successful that almost all other manufacturers adopted it within a year!

Keppel Gate, Isle of Man, 1930

1948

350cc Velocette Mk VIII KTT

In the 1930s, the 350cc ohc Velocette racers were almost invincible, and by the end of the decade, continuous development had resulted in the MkVIII KTT . It was a tough machine with the novelty of swinging arm rear suspension and a top speed of well over 100mph. Unfortunately, the intervention of WWII, and post-War concentration on the LE roadster, meant that very few MkVIII KTTs were made. Because of its revised priorities the factory actually stopped production of the KTT in 1950, and did not even officially support racing at that time, but the sohc single was still a force to be reckoned with in private hands. Riding one entered by Archers of Aldershot, Bob Foster won the Junior TT in 1947, with Freddie Frith repeating the feat in the following two years' events. The same two riders also monopolised the World Championship in 1949 and 1950. Percy Goodman - who had designed the original KTT years earlier - now re-formed the factory team and produced new works machines, but his illness and premature death soon caused the Race Shop to close again, and that spelt the end for the wonderful overhead camshaft Velocettes.

MOTO STORICHE
IN GRAND PRIX
24-25 GIUGNO
1989
misano
adriatico

Velocette

VERDEL

1912
750cc Verdel Radial Five

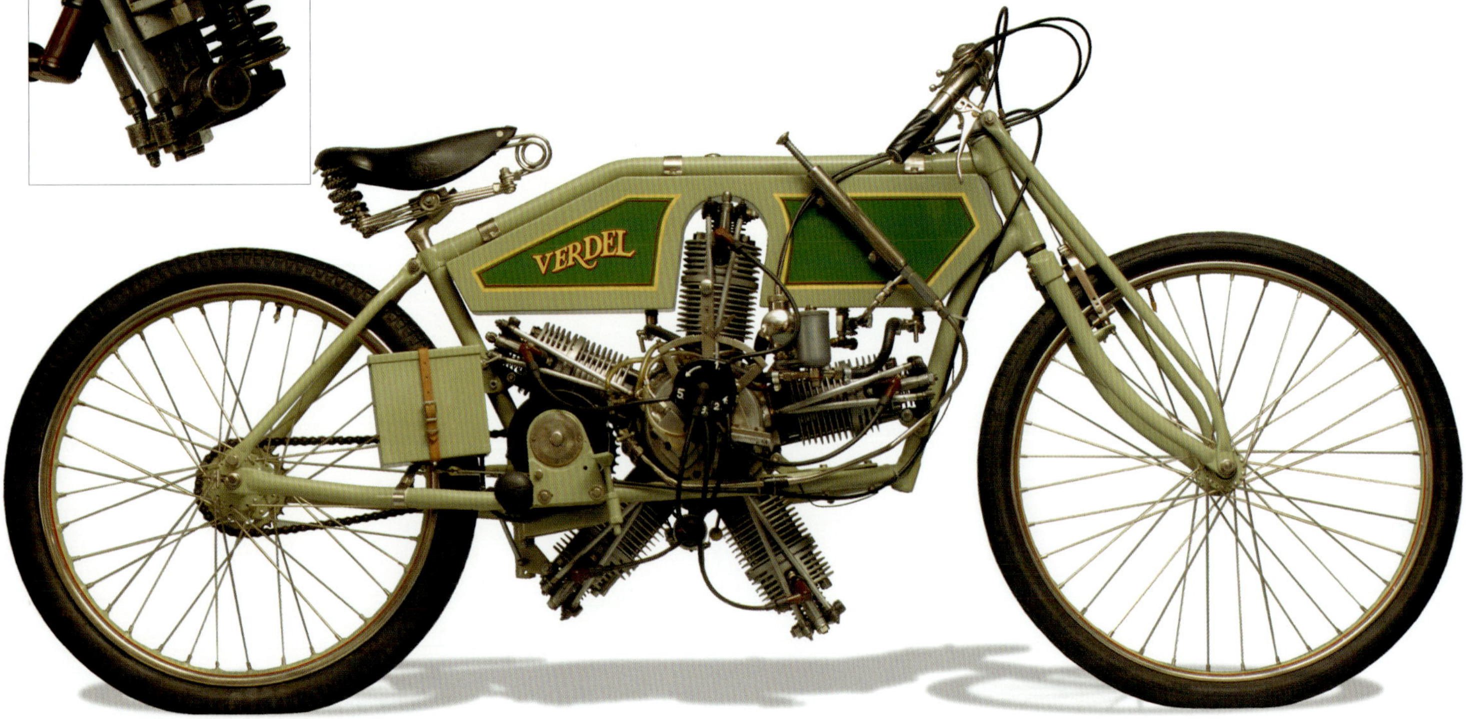

The Verdel is a unique representative of an extremely unfortunate marque, whose primary business was a Peugeot agency in Northern France. Firstly Verdel's paperwork was lost during a WWI bombardment, and then the premises and any subsequent records were destroyed during WWII. The Museum's motorcycle presumably started life in the Verdel workshops, and has doubtless since been updated with features like chain drive, but it was virtually unknown before its sensational emergence at the Millennium Montlhéry Coupes Moto Legende, after which Sammy Miller purchased and restored it in time for demonstration at the opening of his Museum's extension. The author has also had the chance to assess this remarkable device, and found that the enormous five-cylinder radial engine that dominates its appearance also dictates its behaviour, as there is no gearbox, the brakes have negligible effectiveness, and the frame is primitive with no suspension at either end. It seems probable that the Verdel was never intended for use on the open road, and – having reportedly clocked over 80mph at Montlhéry - may well have been prepared as a board racer or a cycle pacing machine. The only certainty is that you won't see a similar machine anywhere else!

c1950
1000cc Series C Vincent Black Shadow Racer

The Series B one-litre Rapide twins announced by Phil Vincent in 1945 created a sensation. In the era of rigid frames and staid single-cylinder commuters, they had full suspension and a top speed of over the magic 'ton'. Two years later, a larger carburettor and a higher compression ratio produced the Black Shadow with a top speed of 120mph. And another two years saw the introduction of an even faster racing version called the Black Lightning, equipped with TT Amal carburettors, and stripped of road-going fitments. The Black Lightning was so exclusive (only 30 were made) and expensive (costing as much as a small house) that if a clubman wanted to go racing in the occasional unlimited capacity race, his usual course of action was to strip and tune a Rapide or Black Shadow. Since it has black engine cases, the Museum's Vincent evidently started life as one of the latter, but it has been expertly and neatly converted, with all the correct touches like lightened and polished controls and brackets. In the right hands such machines were unbeatable, as proved by their three-year monopoly of the short-lived 1000cc Clubman's TT series.

VINCENT

VINCENT
VINCENT

1980
500cc Yamaha TZ

At the end of the 1970s, Yamaha was riding high after Kenny Roberts' three successive World Championships. But those successes had been achieved with a square four two-stroke that was way beyond the reach of anybody except the works-riders. Less well-funded racers had long-since been relying on the TD/TZ 250 and 350cc twins in the smaller classes, but the advent of the F750 Championship opened up another avenue for Yamaha and their customers. Initially, the larger twin was doubled up to make the across-the-frame engine of the TZ750A (with an actual capacity of 700cc) but later on it was overbored to give the full allowable capacity, and a works version of the TZ750 (re-designated the OW31) gave Giacomo Agostini his last racing victory; at Hockeheim in 1977. That model effectively became redundant when the FIM axed the F750 series in 1980, but doubling up the 250cc twin in the same way allowed Yamaha to produce the TZ500cc production racer. While no match for the full-works machines, its top speed of around 180mph made it a formidable competitor, and the Museum's TZ500 is the actual one on which Donny Robinson gained an impressive 2nd place in the 1981 Senior TT.

YAMAHA

1962
250cc Ariel 'Golden' Sports Arrow

Ariel's fully enclosed twin-cylinder two-stroke Leader of 1958 was an instant hit, but wasn't as successful as hoped, because those who wanted weather protection mostly didn't buy motorcycles. Ariel responded by stripping away the bodywork, and in 1960 presented a very different looking sportster called the Arrow. In truth, it wasn't much quicker than the identically-engined Leader, but it looked sporty, and that was all-important when selling to young impressionable riders. Fortunately, the Arrow had exemplary handling, and when Michael O'Rourke came 7th in the 1960 Lightweight TT on one tuned by two-stroke guru Hermann Meier, the scene was set for a real sports version. This appeared in 1961, and although the engine changes didn't amount to much more than a larger carburettor feeding new high-compression cylinder heads with squish-band combustion chambers, the output was boosted by several horsepower, giving a top speed of around 80mph. Equally importantly, the Sports Arrow's glamorous finish instantly allowed it to be given the same evocative nickname as a currently renowned express train. With learners recently being restricted to 250cc motorcycles, there were very few teenagers who didn't put the 'Golden Arrow' right at the top of their wish list.

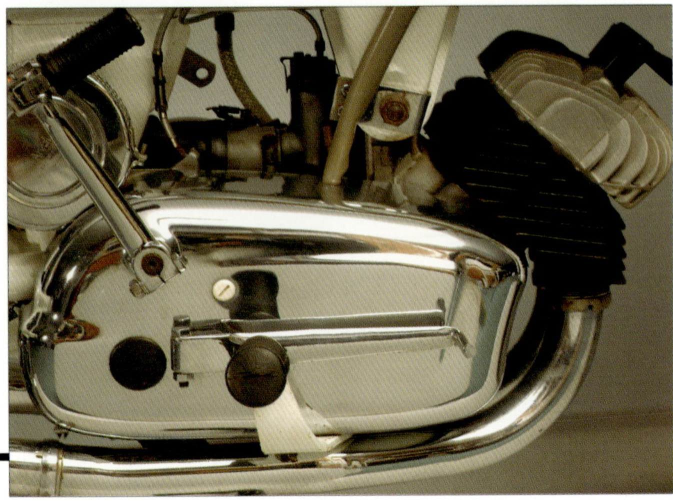

Suggested 1964 ARIEL 'STREET SCRAMBLER' 250c.c. Twin

744 FON

744 FON

c1928
1000cc Brough Superior SS100

The Brough Superior was so highly regarded that when advertised as the 'Rolls Royce of Motorcycles', the car makers did not disagree. Its reputation was partly due to the publicity genius of George Brough who was no mean competitor himself - winning nearly every sprint entered on his own machine – but he cleverly also ensured that his machines would be exploited by famous racers like Eric Fernihough and Noel Pope. George initially helped his father make Brough motorcycles, but set up on his own after WWI and shrewdly added 'Superior' to the family name. The Nottingham concern's most prestigious product was the SS100, introduced in 1924, the number indicating its almost unbelievable top speed. Its rarity (less than 400 were made) and astronomical price tag gave it an almost mythical reputation that paradoxically increased further after national hero Lawrence of Arabia died while riding one. Detractors have always been keen to point out that all production Brough Superiors were really assemblages of appropriate proprietary components, but the Museum's SS100 shows that the result can be more than the sum of the parts, and in terms of style, speed and elegance, what George Brough achieved really was superior.

1929
680cc Brough Superior

So much attention has always been focussed on George Brough's extravagant show-models and road burners, that one tends to forget the 500cc, 680cc and 750cc twins that he made alongside the SS80 and SS100 range-toppers. The engines chosen for the less-publicised motorcycles naturally affected their price, that didn't make them affordable by anybody except the super-rich, as they were finished to the same superlative standard as the bigger machines. The museum's ohv 680cc Sportster, for example, cost around £120 when new, and in 1929 that sum would have bought a decent car, or gone a fair way towards the purchase of a modest house. The smaller models shared all the important features of the one-litre motorcycles, including their superb Castle forks, and had similarly magnificent rounded petrol tanks with aesthetically symmetrical twin filler caps. They didn't give away much in performance, either, as the ohv 680 was almost as fast as the side-valve SS80. It was, however, a couple of inches shorter and weighed about 20lbs less, so if a small enthusiast with a very large wallet wanted the 'Rolls Royce' of motorcycles, this was his machine of choice.

1958
500cc BSA DBD34 Gold Star

Arguably the most charismatic post-War British motorcycle, the DBD34 BSA Gold Star attracts admiration from riders and onlookers alike. In fact, the model had always enjoyed a high profile, as it was a development of the 1937 M23 Empire Star that sensationally earned Walter Handley a Gold Star medal for lapping Brooklands at over 100mph. After the War the Gold Star was initially catalogued as a 350cc all-rounder for the clubman, but then Harold Clark won the 1949 Clubman's TT, and the Gold Star began to be re-oriented towards serious competition duty. In 1950 a 500cc version appeared, and although it was less successful in races than the 350cc Gold Star - which monopolised its class of the Clubman's TT to the extent that it ceased to be of interest – it was the larger variant that attracted most attention, especially when fully kitted out with close ratio gearbox, clip-on handlebars, and the famous silencer that 'twittered' on the overrun. By 1958, the Goldie, as it had became known, was nominally only being made to special order for competition, but most were actually used on the road by 'ton-up kids' who revered its combination of looks and performance.

15·KVO

1962
650cc BSA Rocket Gold Star

BSA's Gold Star never sold in great numbers, but axing its manufacture, and simultaneously introducing featureless unit-construction twins, left BSA's sales list lacking charisma. Even the range-topping Super Rocket had such understated styling – including a staid headlamp nacelle that it shared with the tourers – that it aroused little enthusiasm among fast road riders. But then dealer Eddie Dow, who specialised in 'go-faster' parts for Gold Stars and pre-unit BSA twins, changed everything. What he did was simply to put a Super Rocket engine into a Gold Star frame and add some styling goodies, but that apparently straightforward process magically produced the glamour that BSA's twin had always lacked. A separate headlamp, dropped handlebars, chrome mudguards, better brakes, optional TT carburettor and the fabled close-ratio RRT2 gearbox meant that the machine went as well as it looked, and it looked a million dollars. Dow's Rocket Gold Star was so successful that BSA had little choice but to put it into serial production, and over two thousand were made in a year. Production stopped when the supply of frames and engines dried up, leaving genuine 'Rocket Goldies' as some of the most sought after (and valuable) classic motorcycles ever.

1964
305cc Honda CB77

In 1963, British heavyweights were still justifiably claiming supremacy in the performance stakes when Honda – prompted by American demands – set out to change the situation with its biggest motorcycle yet. The 305cc CB77 (labelled the Super Hawk in the States) had typically angular styling, but its forerunner's pressed steel chassis had been replaced by a tubular steel frame, and its superb specification included a full-width twin leading shoe front brake, and a combined speedometer/tachometer. Following established practice, the single overhead camshaft engine featured 180 degree firing for smoother running, and the twin-carburettors essential with such a design contributed both to street credibility and to an output usually only achieved by half-litre bikes. The CB77 was the first production Honda to have a genuine top speed of more than 100mph, and its combination of performance, good looks and aggressive pricing would surely have taken the market by storm if die-hards had not still been convinced that capacity was all-important. In fact, the Museum's superb CB77 – which was restored by the late Michael Garnett, and donated by his widow Jane - is a rare survivor of a model that was an important step in Honda's evolution.

305cc Honda CB77 donated by Jane Garnett

1957
500cc BSA Gold Star Flat Tracker

During the 1950s the BSA Gold Star gradually evolved into distinct scrambles and racing (or fast road) variants, and there was also an expensive touring version that was seldom seen. All were currently under threat because they were hand-built at a loss, while their mass-produced Triumph stablemates were coining it. However, Gold Stars were still so sought after in America that not only did they need to be kept in production, but there had to be special versions to suit Stateside sport. A slightly modified scrambler (renamed the Catalina) sufficed for the well-known desert races, but something quite different was required for Flat Track races, held on large outdoor circuits with smooth natural surfaces. The primary requirements were considerable power, good handling, and minimal weight. The Gold Star already had the first two attributes, so development of the export-only BSA Flat Tracker involved removing anything not essential, and that included rear suspension, much of the mudguarding, and even the brakes! The late John Gardner - the acknowledged Gold Star expert - restored this factory-made Flat Tracker, and his widow Wendy has loaned it to the Museum where Sammy thoroughly enjoys demonstrating it on appropriate Open Days.

1964
125cc Honda CB92 Benly Super Sport

The Benly spearheaded Honda's assault on western markets, and could not have been more different from contemporary British commuters with their two-stroke engines and three-speed gearboxes. The Benly had a pressed-steel frame, and a twin-cylinder overhead camshaft unit-construction engine with four gear ratios. It also had engine revs previously only heard on the racetrack, a fact that was emphasised by Honda advertisements pointing out the machine's relationship to the 125cc racers that had won the manufacturers' team prize at the previous year's TT. There were actually two Benly models, the C92 roadster with voluminous mudguards, and the CB92 Super Sports, as seen in the Museum, with styling that was much more to British tastes. Admittedly it was expensive, costing more than a BSA with twice the capacity, but its engine was exquisitely made from high-quality aluminium castings, and its comprehensive specification included large full-width brakes. It not only looked like a racer on the road, but it went like one, and if equipped with the optional tuning pack had an output of 15bhp at an stratospheric 10,500rpm, giving a top speed of over 80mph. Sceptics naturally predicted that neither the machines nor the company would last. How wrong they were!

1967
250cc Honda CL72 Street Scrambler

Honda was always alert to new market niches, and in the early-1960s wasted no time exploiting the American-led fashion for giving off-road styling to road-going motorcycles. Cross-country racing fans mostly didn't have the skill or desire to actually compete, but they still wanted their street-legal motorcycles to emulate the looks of the racers, and the Street Scrambler was the result. Honda's first take on the theme was the 1962 CL72, available on both sides of the Atlantic, which initially appeared to be little more than a CB72 sports roadster with sexily upswept exhaust pipes. Study of the Museum's machine – restored by the late Mike Garnett – shows that the changes were more than skin-deep, however, as the new machine had a full loop frame based on that of the RC70 scrambler produced four years earlier, and other sensible features included fork gaiters, a smaller petrol tank and simpler mudguards. With its substantial weight and modest wheel and tyre sizes, the CL72 was obviously more capable on the road than off, but Honda predicted that most buyers would want it that way, and the continually expanding numbers of scrambler-styled machines seen in everyday use shows that their prediction was spot-on.

250cc Honda CL72 Street Scrambler donated by Jane Garnett

1953
175cc FB Mondial TV Sports

FB Mondial was founded in 1935 by the four Boselli brothers (FB standing for Fratelli Boselli) and until WWII they dealt in CM and GD motorcycles. Always interested in sport, the brothers naturally came into contact with GD's star rider Alphonso Drusiani, and younger brother Giuseppe won a Silver Medal in the 1935 ISDT riding a CM. After the war Giuseppe Boselli took charge of the company and tasked Ing (engineer) Drusiani with the design of an FB Mondial racing motorcycle. Within a few months he had devised a dohc 125cc racer that was instantly successful, and it sired a line whose famous riders would later include Sammy Miller. Mondial then began to manufacture roadsters like the TV Sports with a very sporting character, and while its single overhead camshaft engine only had a capacity of 175cc, it had an output of 18bhp giving a top speed of around 80mph. That was astonishing performance to find in a small roadster in the early-1950s, and many Sports Mondials were predictably stripped for racing. The Museum's example, however, has been restored to full road trim, and shows the extraordinary extent to which many Italian manufacturers managed to combine speed, style and sophistication.

F.B
Mondial

1955
200cc FB Mondial Super Sports

Like several other Italian companies, FB Mondial began making motorcycles in response to increased demand for personal transport after WWII. The Bologna-based concern first gained recognition and publicity with a world-beating dohc racer, and then began manufacturing roadsters in a range that quickly expanded to include two-stroke mopeds, plus ohv and ohc four-stroke motorcycles of various capacities from 90 to 250cc. All were lightweights in terms of capacity, but they were never built down to a price. For example, the Museum's 200cc Super Sports is one of the more ordinary models by FB Mondial's standards, yet it has a superb eight-inch front brake, and its pushrod ohv engine is cloaked in beautiful aluminium castings that could easily fool the casual observer into thinking that it had twin shaft-driven overhead camshafts. Its 70mph top speed would easily see off any contemporary British motorcycle in its class, and with a fully duplex frame directly related to that used on the racers it was one of the best looking and most capable lightweight roadsters of its generation. Such quality was inevitably expensive, so exports were minimal, yet FB Mondial managed to continue making its very classy motorcycles until 1969.

1925
1000cc Model ST1 Grindlay Peerless

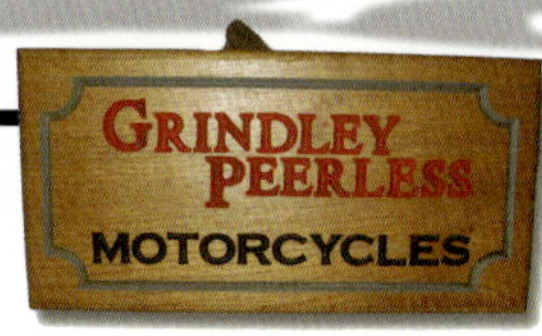

The Model ST1 is the biggest and most expensive of the machines made by the Coventry-based Grindlay family, and it is also one of the most interesting vintage motorcycles ever made. At its heart is the Barr and Stroud sleeve-valve engine, made by a Scottish engineering firm better known for scientific and optical instruments. The principle of this engine is that a movable cylinder liner (the sleeve) sits between the piston and the cylinder wall, and it is mechanically moved so that openings in it line up with cylinder ports at appropriate times to control induction and exhaust. The result is a four-stroke that is as neat and quiet as a two-stroke, in total contrast to contemporary competitors with their exposed and poorly lubricated valvegear. The Museum's ST1 is the only known example of its type, and its overall design is extraordinarily well-balanced and elegant considering that this was one of the earliest Grindlay motorcycles. Reporting on it in Classic MotorCycle magazine, the author found that its attractiveness and mechanical benefits were matched by zestful performance, and when Sammy rode it – newly restored – in the 2008 Banbury Run, it was unsurprisingly awarded the Sheldon Trophy for most technical interest.

1939
1000cc HRD-Vincent Series A Rapide

It is undoubtedly a myth that the inspiration for the pre-War HRD-Vincent twins came from the accidental overlaying of two drawings of the single-cylinder engine, since all prestige manufacturers aimed to include a vee-twin in their range. But designer Phil Irving certainly used elements of the previous design in the twin Rapide unveiled in October 1936. They included a high camshaft position and relatively short stroke, which encouraged the delivery of higher revs and an incomparable power output. Naturally, the new big twin featured Vincent's trademark triangulated swing fork rear suspension, but what set it apart was an astonishing108mph top speed that enabled new advertisements to boast: 'The World's Fastest Standard Motor Cycle - This is a fact, not a slogan!' Of course, the Rapide was ultra-expensive, and acknowledged problems included inadequate transmission, and a leak-prone lubrication system that led to the twins' 'Plumbers' Nightmare' nickname. As a result, only about eighty Series A Rapides were made; so the Museum's survivor is rare and ultra-valuable. The author is lucky enough to have sampled it, and concluded that its combination of appearance, performance, handling and comfort was still unbeaten when the British motorcycle industry collapsed a quarter of a century later.

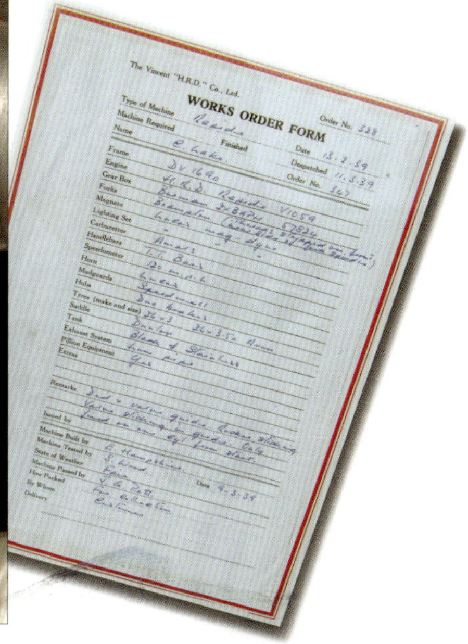
The Vincent "H.R.D." Co., Ltd.

WORKS ORDER FORM

Order No. 328
Type of Machine
Machine Required Rapide
Name C. Lake.
Finished Date 13.2.39
Despatched 11.3.39
Order No. 347
Frame DV1690
Engine
Gear Box
Forks
Magneto
Lighting Set
Carburettor
Handlebars
Speedometer T.T. Bars
Horn 120 m.p.h
Mudguards
Hubs
Tyres (make and size)
Saddle
Tank
Exhaust System
Pillion Equipment
Extras
Remarks
Issued by
Machine Built by
Machine Tested by
State of Weather
Machine Passed by
How Packed Date 9.3.39
By Whom
Delivery

1935
500cc Series A Meteor

Post-War motorcyclists inevitably associate the HRD-Vincent marque with vee-twins, but almost all pre-war models had single cylinder engines. Initially more interested in frames than engines, Phil Vincent, while still an engineering student at Cambridge, built his first special with a sprung rear end and in 1927 began making motorcycles with the prestigious HRD initials added to his own name. The triangulated swinging fork rear suspension worked well but it wasn't what the market wanted, and sales were negligible before the arrival of Australian motorcycle engineer Phil Irving, who was instrumental in the design of attractive new models in 1931. JAP proprietary engines were used until a faulty batch caused the ignominious retirement of the company's entire racing team at the 1934 Senior TT, and then Irving and Vincent designed and built entirely new engines in time for the Motor Cycle Show just four months later. The new Meteor and Comet models proved to have exceptional performance, even the base model having a top speed of over 80mph. Never mass-produced, few pre-War examples survive, and although the Museum's Meteor is one of the earliest, it has all the performance, looks and specification that soon resulted in cult status for all HRD-Vincents.

1965
Honda RC181 Hailwood Replica

Honda was known for its smaller capacity racers until 1965, when the 500cc four cylinder RC181 was unveiled in a direct challenge to the all-conquering MV Agusta. It was probably the expectation that the new machine would dominate the Blue Riband class that lured Mike Hailwood away from MV - for whom he had won the title three years in succession - but it wasn't to be. Giacomo Agostini was now team leader at MV with the recently introduced three-cylinder racer, and its compactness and sure-footedness made up for the extra horsepower of the Honda, whose handling was described as 'evil' by Hailwood. Coming a close second to 'Ago' in the 1966 title race, he had a special frame made for his RC181, but was not allowed to use it, and he again just missed out on the title despite several GP wins and a lap record in the Senior TT. Disappointed, Hailwood temporarily quit the sport, and - upset by FIM decisions favouring two-strokes - Honda quit GP racing too. Despite Hailwood's criticism, the RC181 represents a peak period in Honda's racing history, and Sammy Miller thoroughly enjoys giving the Museum's replica a spirited outing in classic events.

Sammy with RC181 Replica at the Museum

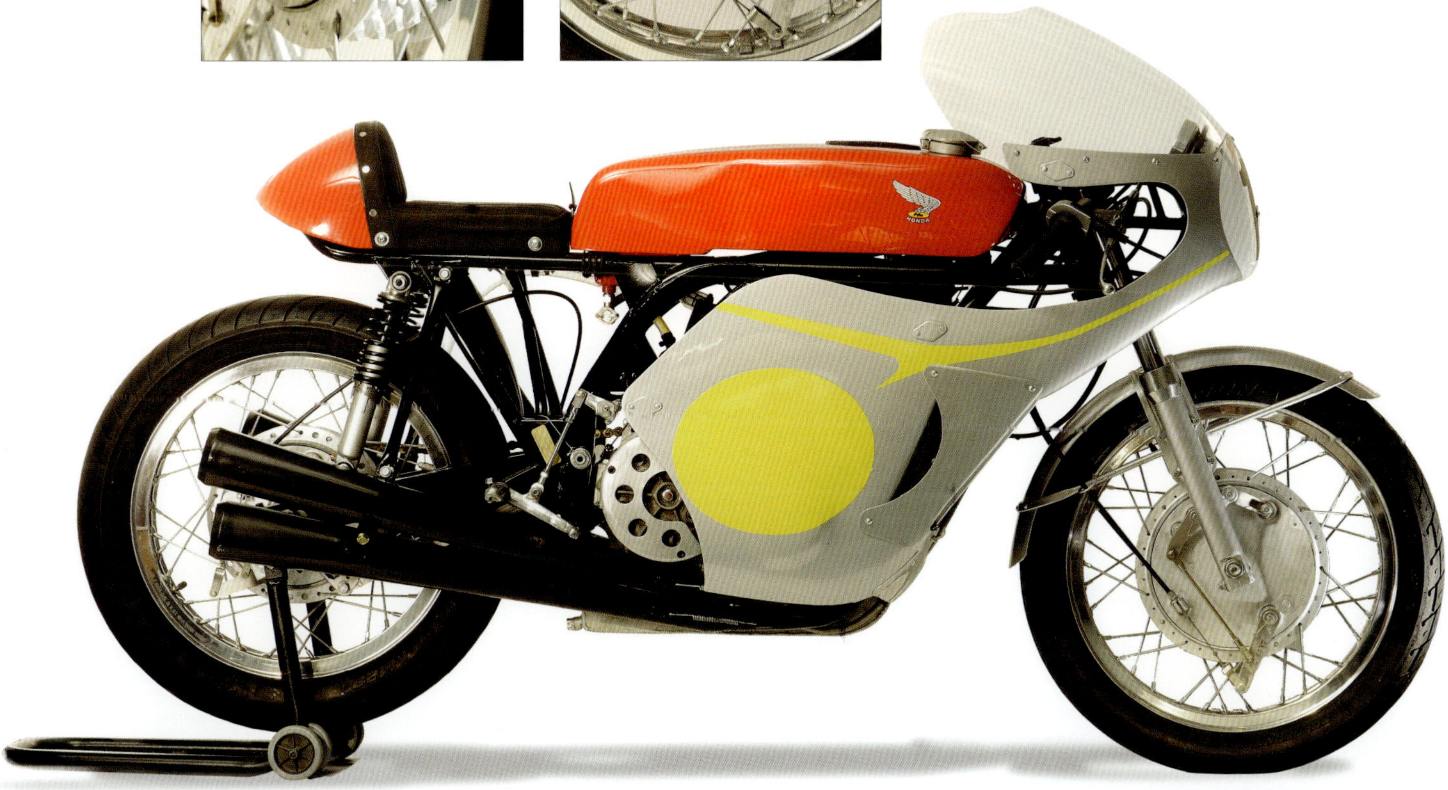
HONDA

c1962
500cc Matchless G50

Although post-War AJS and Matchless roadsters built by Associated Motor Cycles were virtually identical behind their tank badges, the two marques' racing departments initially went their separate ways. The 350cc AJS 7R 'Boy Racer' was introduced in 1948, and its design was sound enough for it to remain successful during steady development throughout the 1950s. Meanwhile, the Matchless G45 - a race-tuned version of the 500cc G9 roadster twin – came and went, and it was 1958 before AMC Ltd took the obvious step of stretching the 7R's engine to produce the 500cc Matchless G50. Its straightforward specification included a duplex frame that housed an engine with a chain-driven single overhead camshaft operating conventional rockers and valves controlled by AMC's usual hairpin springs. Seldom quite as quick as the rival Manx Norton, and lacking its 'Unapproachable' handling, the G50 nevertheless often proved more suitable for short circuit races and was chosen by many stars of the period. The G50 was axed in 1962, but the story didn't end there, as racer and frame builder Colin Seeley bought the entire race shop when AMC collapsed four years later, and he continued making these tough and reliable racers for several years more.

1938
500cc Norton International Model 30

The Norton Internationals of the 1930s were true 'Racers on the Road', and were direct developments of the overhead camshaft motorcycles developed by Arthur Carroll, after Walter Moore (and his designs) had departed for NSU. Carroll's 350cc Model 40 and 500cc Model 30 Internationals were first supplied to the Works team in 1930, and in 1931 they dominated both TT classes, a feat that was surpassed the following year when they took all the podium places in both categories, and won ten Continental GPs in a row. Internationals then became available to private motorcyclists, and since they could be used on the road or track, they were normally provided with full road equipment. From 1936 onwards, however, Internationals supplied specifically for racing began to divert from the road machines, and they were given many upgrades including better oiling, lumpier camshaft profiles, bigger carburettors and racing magnetos. Development tailed off towards the end of the decade as Bracebridge Street geared up for military contracts, so the Museum's Model 30 represents the peak of the International's early development. The 'Inter' was catalogued again after WWII, but it was now purely a fast roadster, and its racing days were history.

1957
350cc Manx Norton Model 40M

The Manx Norton evolved from the International, and its name was derived from the 'Manx Grand Prix Inters' supplied to semi-works riders in 1939. Introduced as the 350cc Model 40M and 500cc Model 30M in 1947, the early Manxes were essentially pre-War motorcycles up-dated with telescopic forks. With limited works opposition they continued winning, but by 1950 the writing was on the wall, despite painstaking engine development by race chief Joe Craig. Luckily however, the Manx was then given a new lease of life by the adoption of the Featherbed Frame, developed in Ireland as a private venture by the McCandless brothers and Artie Bell. Coincidentally, Norton engaged Geoff Duke – the best rider of his generation – as works rider, and the rest is history. Throughout the 1950s, the Manx was simply the best over-the-counter racer available, and it served a multitude of aspiring and established riders. By the end of the decade, Norton publicity could claim without fear of contradiction that the Manx was, 'The most successful standard production racing machine in the world'. Factory production ceased in 1962, but enthusiasts wouldn't let the Manx Norton die, and replicas are still being produced and raced to this day.

MANX
Norton
MODEL 40M
348cc. 1957

Norton

THE
OR CYCLE
EVERY
THURSDA
8

Sammy getting in some practice on a 350cc Manx Norton at the 1956 Ulster GP.

1973
350cc Yamaha TZ

YAMAHA

Yamaha's 1972 works racers - on which Jarno Saarinen almost pulled off the 250/350cc World Championship double - were effectively the prototypes for the following year's production racers to be designated the TZ250 and TZ350. These six-speed liquid-cooled machines were front runners from the start, with Saarinen winning three 250cc GP rounds in a row, and taking the bigger TZ – as seen in the Museum - to victory in the Daytona 200 and Imola 200 races, competing against top European superbikes with much greater capacities. Tragically, Saarinen was killed mid-season, but the TZ350 continued its winning ways in the 1974 World Championship when it was ridden by ex-MV Agusta star Giacomo Agostini, and ironically, his main opponent was Phil Read, who had taken his place on the MV. The following year – when Agostini concentrated on the bigger classes –Johnny Cecotto took his place as lead TZ350 rider and duly took over as 350cc World Champion. At the end of the year, Yamaha announced reduced support for the works riders, but development of the TZ models continued, the essential excellence of the design being confirmed when the twins were doubled up to make the world-beating TZ500/700.

YAMAHA

1966
650cc Norton 650SS

Norton didn't apply the Dominator name to their range-topping 650SS in the early-1960s, but it was effectively the latest model in a line stretching back to 1951, when the existing half-litre twin engine was fitted into the new Featherbed frame. By 1960 the engine's capacity had been increased to match the best on offer from the BSA/Ariel/Triumph conglomerate, and in response to complaints from shorter riders the top frame rails had been brought closer together to make the 'Slimline' frame. The changes enhanced the elegant and purposeful lines of the range, and the addition of twin downdraught carburettors was the finishing touch on the 650 Sports that was announced in 1962. It was as effective as it was handsome, and when local dealer Syd Lawton prepared one for Phil Read and Brian Setchell, they won the next two Thruxton 500mile production races, plus a similar event at Silverstone. The Museum's superb 650SS is on loan from David Joyce, who fully restored it after its discovery in a ditch. It is a measure of the esteem in which the six-fifty Norton was held that it survived the demise of parent company AMC, and continued in production (in single-carburettor form) until 1970.

1924
1000cc Packman and Poppe Sprinter

In the early-1920s Erling Poppe – whose father's company made White and Poppe motorcycle engines - began producing P&P motorcycles in partnership with Gilmour Packman. Poppe's design featured a rigid frame made from virtually straight tubes, with its stiffness maximised by the positive location of the rear wheel spindle in the frame, an unorthodoxy that necessitated moving the entire engine/gearbox assembly to adjust the chain! The first P&Ps used single-cylinder proprietary engines but a JAP vee-twin was soon squeezed into the frame to make a prototype for a production model, and this is the actual machine on display in the Museum. Erling Poppe used it as his personal sprinter, and with its ultra-compact layout, good handling and an exceptional power-to-weight ratio, it was very successful. The same cannot be said of Poppe's company, for during 1925 his partner Packman was killed in a brawl, and the Montgomery motorcycle works – where many P&P components were made - was burnt to the ground. Poppe sold out with production barely started, and the Museum's P&P is the only vee-twin out of four known survivors. Two decades later the visionary, but unlucky, Erling Poppe finally achieved fame as the designer of BSA's shaft-drive Sunbeams.

JAP

HP 5577
JAP

c1959 250cc REG

The REG was arguably the most successful privately-constructed British racer of all time. Its initials stand for Robert (Bob) E Geeson, a highly skilled engineer who began its development around 1949, when he constructed a radical twin cylinder engine with gear-driven double overhead camshafts, and fitted it into a modified Rudge frame. After considerable development the engine was safe to 10,000rpm, and the machine's potential was shown by its creator's tenth place in the 1953 Lightweight TT. The up and coming John Surtees then took over the saddle, and he achieved several wins and lap records before graduating to a works ride with MV Agusta. The original REG was then sold, and Geeson put all that he had learnt into two MkII versions, the surviving example of which has recently been restored for display in the Museum. Many of the top non-works riders of the day campaigned the MkII REG, including John Hartle and Derek Minter, who achieved several short circuit wins during 1958. Other notable riders included Sid Mizen, Chris Vincent and Fred Hardy, whose most impressive result, against full works opposition, was seventh place in the 1962 TT, shortly before the machine was retired.

R.E.G.

R.E.G.

1949
500cc Triumph GP

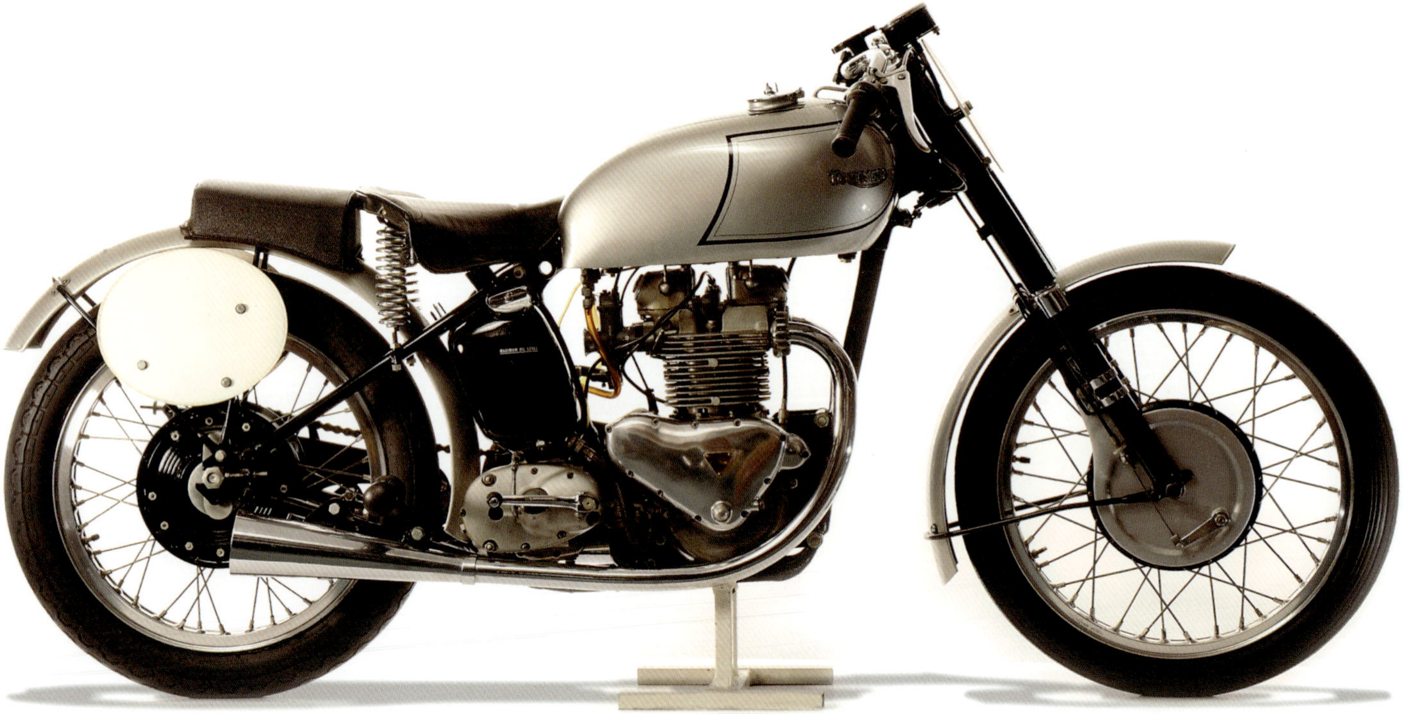

In 1946, Triumph's management abandoned its normal caution and allowed former Brooklands record holder, Freddie Clarke, to prepare a racing version of the Tiger 100. Its standard bottom end was topped off with the aluminium alloy barrels and head from a wartime generator motor, chosen because of better heat conduction, and the frame was given the recently-introduced sprung rear hub. The prototype was tested by Irishman Ernie Lyons in relative obscurity during a 1946 Ulster road race, and was then entered in that year's Manx Grand Prix. Lyons – who had ridden a Triumph Twin in the last Manx GP before the War - was the ideal rider, for he had the strength to hold the indifferently handling Triumph on abysmally wet roads, even after a frame tube broke. He famously won the event, and Triumph was virtually obliged to go into limited production with a replica machine naturally catalogued as the Grand Prix model. Many copies have since been made by enthusiasts, but the Museum's Triumph - with its racing number plate signed by Ernie Lyons himself - is one of about two hundred originals, and is to factory specification except for its front wheel size and unpainted mudguards.

1971
350cc Yamaha TR2

YAMAHA

The prototype TR2 appeared at the 1968 Daytona 200mile. Forced to comply with AMA rules drawn up to favour Harley Davidsons, it only had a four-speed gearbox, but Mike Duff's race speed of 132mph was still enough to see off most of the American twins with more than double the capacity. The gearbox restriction probably benefited Yamaha riders in the long run, because the TR2's developers were forced to provide the piston-ported engine with a 2000rpm-wide power band, and it was usable from 6000-10,000rpm. The TR2 (and its 250cc sibling – the TD2) were put on limited sale in early-1969, making it the first 350cc Yamaha production racer, and the wealthy and/or well-connected riders who managed to get hold of one were presented with a five-speed 54bhp engine that was the equal of everything except the MV four. The Yamaha twin was even competitive in the GPs, with Kel Carruthers managing second place in the 1970 title chase, and Yamaha riders taking the next nine places after Agostini and the 350cc MV in 1971. The Museum's racer marks the final development of the model before it was replaced by the short-lived TR3.

1930
350cc Velocette KSS

The overhead camshaft Model K Velocette racer was announced in 1925, and the KSS (K Super Sports) roadster followed one year later. To be strictly accurate, the first of the K Series should be referred to as Veloce motorcycles, as it was initially intended to reserve the Velocette (or Little Veloce) name for the company's well-regarded two-stroke machines. Indeed, it was partly the desire to move away from the utility reputation of two-strokes that led Percy Goodman to design the new engine. And contrary to the general perception of ohc racers as aggressive oil-spraying devices, he chose the layout primarily because it potentially provided more sophistication than the exposed and poorly lubricated valve gear of contemporary ohv engines. Despite teething troubles (which, ironically, included valve spring breakages and copious oil leaks) he was proved right, and the K Series machines earned a reputation for combining excellent performance with civilised behaviour. The road-going KSS seen in the Museum – restored by David Osborne – was a light and nimble machine, yet it had a guaranteed top speed of 80mph, and with its innovatory four-speed foot-change gearbox, would easily show a clean pair of heels to much bigger and more pretentious machines.

Velocette

1934
350cc Velocette Mk IV KTT

Velocette's overhead camshaft racer was known simply as the Model K when Alec Bennett annihilated the opposition (despite a fall) in the 1926 Junior TT, and it was only after he repeated the win two years later that Veloce Ltd marketed a TT replica with the immortal KTT designation. Superficially similar to the KSS fast roadster, the racer's engine had several special features including a stronger crankcase, and valve gear lubricated by a dedicated oil pump. Internal improvements boosted power, and a KTT became the first 350cc machine to cover more than 100miles in an hour at Brooklands, and it was also the first production machine to benefit from a positive stop gear change. All that was passed on to the customer, and it is no exaggeration to say that the Mk I KTT was the first viable over-the-counter racer. Developments followed quickly, and by 1932 the Mk IV KTT was in production with the cooling of its cylinder head improved by the use of aluminium bronze. The Museum's Mk IV was once owned and ridden by the celebrated Noel Christmas, and on it he won the 1935 Hutchinson 100 Brooklands race at an average speed of over 97mph.

1966
500cc Velocette Thruxton Venom

Veloce Ltd re-introduced their single cylinder MSS in 1954, and while it was no sportster, enthusiasts soon discovered that its engine's short stroke and high camshaft position made it easy to tune. In 1956 the factory responded with the sporty Venom, which soon became so popular that a special Clubman version was produced, and one of these achieved immortality in 1961 with its renowned 100mph/24hours record at Montlhéry. The day of the big single seemed to be over, though, until specialist dealer Reg Orpin used a special cylinder head - developed by Velocette's American importer - on a Venom which promptly won its class in the 1964 Barcelona and Thruxton Production races. Velocette swiftly produced the replica Venom Thruxton, and the fast rider was finally provided with a worthy replacement for the sadly-missed BSA Gold Star. And if the similarity included difficult starting (Sammy Miller remembers Velocette Thruxton riders struggling to get going in endurance races as he shot off on the works Ariel Arrow) that only added to the kudos. Once underway, though, the Thruxton was a superb machine, with looks that matched its speed, handling and braking, and a glorious exhaust note from its fishtail exhaust.

Velocette
GLD 677C

1967
250cc Yamaha TD1C

Yamaha's early production racers were based on the machines used by the everyday rider, which was no surprise considering the unprecedented performance of the YDS roadsters. Much further development went into the engine of the 1962 TD1A, though, and it had a totally new top end, a lighter frame and improved brakes. Unfortunately, the machine's clutch could not reliably cope with the increased power - even though that was rather less than claimed - and in I964 the TD1B appeared with better transmission and another top end. The power was now up to 33bhp at 10,500rpm, and while that was a remarkable output for a piston-ported two-stroke, it was still not fully competitive against the top opposition from Aermacchi et al. Yamaha's engineers went back to work, and in 1967 they came up with the TD1C as seen here. The transmission had been revised and strengthened again, and power was up to 36bhp which was sufficient for Mick Chatterton to achieve sixth place in the 1967 Lightweight TT, while Rod Gould's Bultaco-framed TD1C came third in the season's GP Championship table. Development continued until the end of the decade, when Yamaha introduced the even more powerful and successful TD2.

YAMAHA

YAMAHA
YAMAHA

1972
125cc Yamaha TA125

During the early to mid-1960s, competition between the 'big three' Japanese manufacturers made the 125cc GP class one of the most competitive and innovative, with the honours fairly evenly shared between Honda, Suzuki and Yamaha. By 1967, though, Yamaha was in the ascendant, with 35bhp water-cooled V-fours that allowed Bill Ivy and Phil Read to share the championship honours, a situation that was repeated the following year when Ivy also achieved the first ultra-lightweight 100mph-plus lap of the TT course. With Honda and Suzuki then dropping out of the GP scene, Yamaha could doubtless have carried on winning at will, except that the FIM promptly decreed that future 125cc racers would be restricted to two cylinders and six speeds. The company understandably responded by concentrating more effort on its already successful larger twins, and the smaller machines – even those campaigned by factory riders – became progressively less exciting. By 1970, Yamaha's water-cooled 125cc twins were only producing about 30bhp; and when the air-cooled 1972 TA125 was announced, it was visibly based on the relatively mundane AS3 roadster. Its 24bhp output was impressive enough for a clubman's production racer, perhaps, but it was a far cry from what had been available from the earlier race shop exotica.

YAMAHA

YAMAHA

1950
1000cc Vincent Black Shadow Roadster

The awesome performance of the post-War Series 'B' Rapide wasn't enough for Vincent employee George Brown who was already a well-known racer and sprinter. With help from his brother Cliff, and designer Phil Irving, he took a Rapide that had been rejected by the Test Department and transformed it into 'Gunga Din', which became almost invincible in sprints, hill climbs and races. Company boss Phil Vincent was convalescing from a motorcycle crash at the time, but when he returned to work he applied some of George Brown's tuning tips to a production motorcycle, and the result was the most impressive Vincent roadster of them all. Christened the Black Shadow, its unique black crankcases made it instantly recognisable, and by 1950 when the Museum's C Series machine was made, Vincent's own equally distinctive 'Girdraulic' forks had replaced the old-fashioned Brampton girders used previously. Lusted after by almost all motorcyclists, but only affordable by a tiny minority, the Black Shadow nevertheless remained in production until 1954 with trend-setting styling that included straight handlebars and polished aluminium mudguards. Not until the late-1960s would any other British motorcycle come close to challenging its output of 55bhp and top speed of more than 120mph.

VINCENT

VINCENT

1964
350cc AJS 16C Trials

Post-War AJS and Matchless single-cylinder machines were firmly, and logically, based on the Matchless G3L that had performed so well on the battlefield. As enthusiasts had come to expect, there was great similarity between the two marques' products, and also between the 350cc and 500cc options. In fact, there wasn't even much difference between the 1945 roadsters and the scrambles/trials machines announced one year later, the off-road modifications amounting to little more than differently sized wheels with knobbly tyres, slightly lowered gearing, aluminium mudguards (still painted black) and upswept exhausts. And, apart from the competition engines being given an alloy top end in 1950, and buyers having the option of springing after 1951, that was pretty much how they stayed. But that was normal in an era when clubmen still expected to ride trials machines to work during the week, and the AMC motorcycles were extraordinarily successful despite their conservative specification. Top riders Hugh Viney and Gordon Jackson won numerous events on them throughout the 1950s, their achievements crowned by the latter's famous one-mark victory, just beating Sammy in the 1961 SSDT. Many riders were already turning to lightweight two-strokes, and the Museum's neat AJS represents the end of an honourable line.

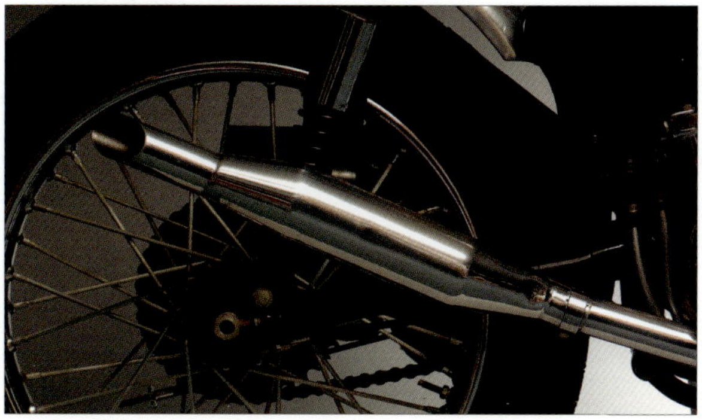

1957
500cc Ariel HT5 Trials

Modern motorcyclists might well wonder why the Ariel HT5's maker and original customers were content with a machine so closely related to the Red Hunter roadster. But the average rider simply didn't have the money to buy specialised machines, and if that made his motorcycle a jack of all trades, rather than master of one, that's just the way things were. And with that proviso in mind, the early Competition Hunters were pretty effective machines. Like the rest of the single cylinder range they were descended from the wartime W/NG, but in some respects – such as their aluminium alloy cylinder heads and barrels – they were more advanced than the roadsters. By the mid-1950s still more specialisation was needed, and the general purpose 500cc competition machine was replaced by dedicated scramblers and triallers with new swinging arm frames. The trials motorcycle was available in 350cc or 500cc form (designated HT3 and HT5 respectively) and it was one of the latter that introduced the young Sammy Miller to the marque in 1956. As is well known, he developed it out of all recognition, but the production machine seen in the Museum changed little before it was discontinued two years later.

GOV 132
500cc Ariel Trials

In the late 1950s and early-1960s, the name Sammy Miller was invariably associated with a very special trials motorcycle bearing the registration plate GOV 132. Sammy was first acquainted with that registration when he was loaned an Ariel HT5 just before the 1956 Scottish Six Days Trial. Having previously been used to riding diminutive two-strokes, he was taken aback by the machine's size and weight, but proved himself equal to the challenge with a Special First Class Award. Promptly invited to join Ariel's Competition Department, Sammy modified GOV 132 with a minimal exhaust and Ariel Leader hubs, and fettled it into a regular trials winner. Other companies might have cashed in with a Sammy Miller replica, but Ariel had decided to finish with four-strokes, selling GOV 132 to Sammy for one pound in 1960. That bargain purchase allowed him scope for development outside factory policy, and eventually his motorcycle weighed a mere 245lbs with his own design of frame and glass fibre bodywork. Sammy continued to win cup after cup, but he was swimming against the tide, and in 1964 he made the momentous decision to retire the 'Most famous trials machine in the World', while he continued his winning ways on a lightweight two-stroke.

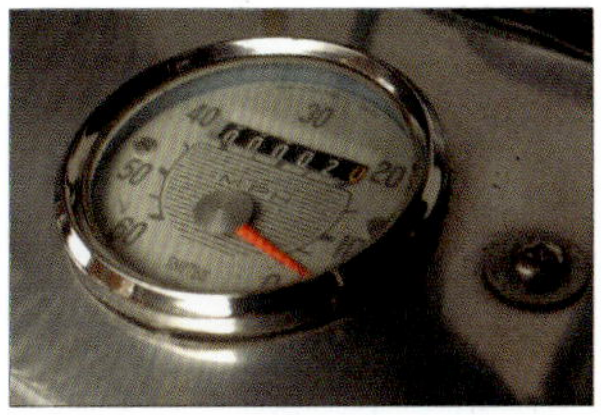

ARIEL
SAMMY MILLER

Sammy at the Scottish Six Days Trial 1962, Grey Mare's Ridge

Sammy with GOV 132 at the start of the 1962 Scottish Six Days Trial, which he won

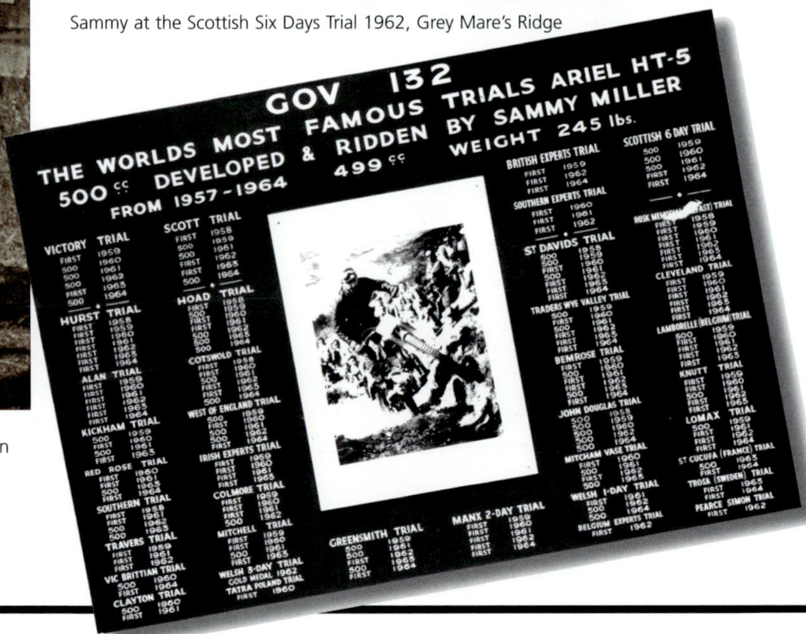

Scottish Six Days Trial, Loch Eala Path, GOV 132, 1959

1964
250cc Bultaco Sherpa

Two-stroke triallers had been ascendant for years, so Sammy Miller's 1964 defection from the four-stroke ranks would not have made headline news if he hadn't still been almost invincible on GOV 132, and if he hadn't switched to a virtually unknown marque. But the wins had been as much due to Sammy's abilities as those of his obsolescent Ariel, and now he had the unprecedented offer of a completely new motorcycle, plus the full support of its maker. During a secret visit to Spain, Sammy had made many modifications to an ISDT Bultaco, whose engine was bored out from its previous 196cc, and after intensive testing alongside the Ariel, he felt that it could be a winner. And so it proved; the very next day after a last victorious ride on GOV 132, a Bultaco Sherpa like the one in the Museum enabled Sammy to notch up the first of innumerable wins he would achieve during a happy ten year association with Señor Bulto. Further development by Sammy quickly turned the Sherpa into the clubman's favourite mount, and lightweight foreign machines like this soon became so capable that pre-65 trials were introduced to provide a competitive outlet for older British motorcycles.

BULTACO

BULTACO

Scott Trial, 1967

Sammy at the Trader's Cup Trial, 1970, on the Bultaco

1953
DOT Model T (Trials)

Among the many British firms producing Villiers-engined lightweights after WWII, DOT was unusual in making off-road competition motorcycles right from the start. The focus was initially on scramblers - one of which was raced by the young Sammy Miller before he left Ireland – but a trials machine joined the range in 1951. Like its immediate competitors, it had a rigid frame, plus a three-speed 197cc engine, and - weighing in at a mere 190lbs - it was soon winning awards for its owners. In 1953 DOT took the forward-looking step of supplementing the trialler's Metal Profile telescopic front forks with swinging arm rear suspension, and it was a well-thought out design where the Girling units were mounted well forward to enhance the wheel's movement. The new machine could well have become the class leader if DOT had straightaway set up a works team, but by the time they engaged Eric Adcock in 1954, other machines were similarly improved. Adcock and team mates like Doug Theobold performed valiantly, but DOT never quite hit the big time. However, by concentrating on its sturdy and capable off-road machines the Manchester company survived longer than many competitors, eventually closing its doors in 1970.

1963
250cc 24 TES Greeves Scottish

The Greeves Scottish was named in honour of Jack Simpson's class win in the 1957 Scottish Six Days Trial, and for many years it was the clubman trials rider's favourite. The Scottish went through a large number of updates during its eight year production span, each change being indicated by a different suffix letter after the 'T' (Trials). The TE was introduced in 1962, and its frame – which still featured Greeves' trademark alloy beam frame and rubber front suspension - was specially devised for trials, in contrast to previous models which had shared the scramblers' basic design. More noticeably, the engine had a square-section alloy cylinder barrel, which slightly reduced the weight while significantly increasing the power output. The TE stayed in production for three years, and the 24TES was the top version, the prefix and suffix referring to its 246cc Special engine whose weighted flywheel resulted in increased pulling power. Don Smith won the 1964 European Trials Championship on a Greeves TES, but continental competition was looming in the shape of Sammy Miller's Bultaco. Greeves continued making successful triallers until forced out by the lack of suitable engines, but their fortunes were never quite the same again.

c1976
305cc Honda TL305 Trials

Honda had always concentrated on the high-speed branches of motorcycle sport, so the 1974 news that Sammy Miller had signed a contract to develop a Honda trialler raised almost as many eyebrows as his move to Bultaco ten years earlier. But Honda was known for four-stroke technology that promised the low speed torque so desirable in trials riding, and - after intensive development work by Sammy in Japan and England - the TL250 engine delivered what it promised. Honda's chassis had less to offer, so the engine was fitted into a locally-made frame in the 'Highboy' style already developed by Sammy. The prototype Honda Trials was an immediate winner in his hands, but attempts to put it into production initially resulted in too much bulk and weight. After feedback from New Milton to Honda's R&D Department, however, the engine was made more compact despite an enlarged capacity, and housing it in a frame made entirely to Sammy's specification resulted in an all-up weight of less than 200lbs. Sammy's contract with Honda only lasted for three years, but in that time the Japanese concern was transformed from a producer of indifferent trail bikes to a maker of championship-winning competition machines.

Demonstration, Thruxton Honda Festival, 305 Honda

Non-stop feet-up record, 27 cars, Beaulieu, 1974

1977
402cc ISDT Jawa

Those not in the know tend to disparage all Jawas because of their kinship to the cheap and cheerful two-stroke commuters seen everywhere during the 1960s and 1970s. But Jawa has an honourable history, dating back to 1929, and at times the roadsters have been supplemented by racers, scramblers, grass/dirt trackers, scooters and mopeds. The later International Six Days Trial machines were just about the most successful and prestigious Jawas ever, and that's not surprising as they had decades of ISDT experience behind them. Even during the days when the factory's activities were most severely constrained by its communist rulers, the simple but reliable Czechoslovakian two-strokes had frequently embarrassed better-funded west European teams. When their reliability was supplemented by real power in the 1970s, Jawa's engineers had the comparatively simple task of adding a centre stand and a few road-legal necessities to an already beefy off-road motorcycle, and their riders were presented with a supremely competitive motorcycle. The Museum's example is an actual ex-works machine used to win a Gold Medal in 1977, after which it was sold to the British Army's REME team, to be regularly campaigned by Ted Johns before its final retirement.

JAWA

1953
200cc Greeves Trials

Oscar Bertrum (Bert) Greeves owed his career to the successful motorised wheelchair that he made for his disabled cousin, because that inspired him to establish a factory making invalid carriages for servicemen wounded during WWII. Initially these vehicles used conventional springing, but around 1950 Bert Greeves evolved the concept of fitting them with suspension that relied on rubber in torsion. Like all good ideas, the principle was simple, and involved little more than attaching the outer circumference of a rubber 'doughnut' to the frame, and linking its central bore to a suspension arm – as the arm moved, the rubber 'wound up' creating progressive resistance. Already an enthusiastic rider, Bert experimented with the idea on a two-wheeler, and found it so satisfactory that Greeves motorcycles were soon in production. Reflecting his personal interests, off-road machines were made from the start, and it was quickly found that the friction dampers appropriate to rotary motion were inadequate under competition conditions. By 1955 conventional suspension units were fitted at the rear, and soon afterwards the 'doughnut' springing on the leading link forks was supplemented by hydraulic dampers. The Museum's trialler, however, is a very early and rare example, featuring rubber suspension on both wheels.

1978
310cc Miller-Hiro Trials Prototype

After completing his contract with Honda, Sammy Miller temporarily became involved with SWM, before being approached by Andrea Mosconi of Milan. Signor Mosconi was making the promising 310cc two-stroke Hiro motor, and plans were laid to go into production with it fitted into a Miller trials frame. This was no problem for Sammy, as a decade earlier he had made over four hundred Highboy frames and had actually manufactured about forty-five complete trials machines before the supply of Villiers engines finally dried up. Now he fitted the six-speed Hiro engine into a frame that incorporated his accumulated knowledge, and the result was the prototype seen in the Museum. Unfortunately, a market survey indicated that there would not be enough demand to put it into quantity production, and the project and general design was passed on to Alan Clews, better known for his four-stroke CCM scramblers. In turn, the much larger Armstrong concern acquired CCM, and continued production of the trials motorcycle under its own name. In a neat twist of fate, it was on a Hiro-engined Armstrong - whose origins could be traced directly back to himself - that Sammy notched up his one thousandth trials win.

350
Hiro
Sammy
Miller

Miller
350
Hiro
Sammy
Miller

1949
500cc Norton 500T

Norton was slow to realise that the trials scene had changed after WWII, and its initial offering - with full road-going equipment and close fitting mudguards - was no match for its Ariel and AMC contemporaries. Fortunately, Artie Bell and the McCandless brothers over in Belfast undertook some serious development – as they had with other Norton projects – and Norton re-entered the fray in 1948 with the vastly improved 500T. Its frame was still based on the old 16H type, but abbreviated rear chain stays significantly reduced the wheelbase, and further shortening was achieved by a new bottom fork yoke that steepened the fork angle and sharpened up the steering. The construction appeared conventional enough, but an alloy cylinder barrel and head were specified, and many parts – including the petrol tank, silencer and wheel rims – were made in lighter gauge steel to minimise the weight. Most of Norton's development effort was of course expended on its racing programme, and although a promising youngster named Geoff Duke was recruited specifically for the trials team, he soon switched roles and development of the 500T stagnated. This handsome machine was deleted from the sales list in 1954, and today it is a much sought-after rarity.

1914
1000cc Packer Board Racer

In later years Indian and Harley Davidson came to dominate the American motorcycle industry, but there were innumerable other pioneer manufacturers who hopefully set up businesses and then disappeared almost without trace. One such is Packer, of Penna, Philadelphia, which doesn't even appear in the reference books, and yet – judging by the Museum's unique example – made impressive and technically advanced motorcycles. This particular machine was evidently designed for Board Racing, a peculiarly American sport where monstrous machines raced on enclosed wooden ovals. The consequences of a crash were horrendous for both rider and machine, making the survival of the Packer all the more remarkable. Its specification is equally astonishing, as this veteran racer has an overhead camshaft engine, with three desmodromically operated valves to each cylinder. This system of mechanically closing valves as well as opening them was re-invented decades later by Ducati, but whereas they used it to control valve 'float' at high revs, in the Packer it would have been more valuable in mitigating the effects of valve-spring failure – a frequent occurrence given the current state of metallurgy. Little more is known about the Packer, but it is undoubtedly – as it says on the tank – Special.

SHS

Samuel Hamilton Special Trials Replica

As a young man in Northern Ireland, Sammy Miller decided that the only way he could afford the trials motorcycle he wanted was to build it himself. The basis was an old Matchless frame, and – already confident that he could improve on factory efforts – he shortened and lightened it, as well as altering the geometry. He fitted it with a brand new Villiers 8E engine that he had rebuilt with crankcase 'stuffers' to boost the power, and used his own forenames to christen the result the Samuel Hamilton Special, or SHS for short. Soon Sammy and his machine were winning local trials, and in 1954 he decided to enter the toughest event of all – the Scottish Six Days. With no back-up transport, he had no option but to ride the SHS to the event and to continue carrying his luggage during the competition. He took the Belfast boat to Glasgow then rode to the start in Edinburgh, 1100 miles in the event, then back to Glasgow and home. Winning the Ben Nevis award, best newcomer, made it all worth while. Sadly, the actual machine on which Sammy first honed his riding and developmental abilities has long-since disappeared, but he located a similar frame and created the SHS replica to accompany the other triallers that subsequently benefitted from those skills.

Sammy, aged 17 in his first Scottish Six Days Trial

1929
500cc Model DT5 Speedway Douglas

Douglas was among the first manufacturers to take off-road racing seriously, after its machines had done well in dirt track races in Australia during the 1920s. The flat-twin engine's valve gear was undoubtedly vulnerable to dust and grit, but in compensation the engine layout gave the Douglas a very low centre of gravity, which assisted stability when drifting round corners. By about 1927 the ohv Dirt Track model was in production, and as the Museum's DT5 shows, much care had been taken with its design, a special frame and petrol tank reducing the height to the minimum. Fortunately for Douglas, the fairly constant speeds maintained on speedway tracks only required a single drive ratio that could be achieved with a simple layshaft. If a gearbox had been required, it would have had to be located either behind or above the rear cylinder, and these design solutions would have respectively lengthened or raised the machine to an unacceptable degree. Douglas's supremacy was quickly challenged by other manufacturers such as Rudge, and JAP's unbeatable single cylinder speedway engine which would soon be available to everybody, but for once the West Country manufacturers temporarily benefitted from their perpetual preparedness to try something new.

Douglas.

Simon Wigg's
500cc Jawa Long Tracker

Grasstrack and speedway races both involve power-drifting round fairly short anti-clockwise circuits, but while the motorcycles used appear somewhat similar, grasstrackers have to cope with bumps and irregular corners on a natural surface, while speedway riders need no rear suspension or gearbox to ride at a fairly constant speed on levelled cinders. The two events come together in Long Track Races, where a fairly flat circuit of up to a mile is covered in shale, and speedway-style drifting predominates, even though the surface demands grasstrack-style machines. This branch of the sport is especially popular in Germany, but English riders have often starred, the most successful of all being Simon Wigg. His Long Tracker is typical of the breed with a steep fork angle, enclosed wheels, and a Czechoslovakian-made overhead camshaft Jawa motor, which is laid down to lower the centre of gravity. There are no brakes or unnecessary weight, but there is a two-speed gearbox and basic rear suspension. Simon Wigg gained five World Titles in the years leading up to 1994, but sadly succumbed to a brain tumour while still at his peak, and his family subsequently entrusted his championship-winning Long Track machine to the Museum Trust.

JAWA
898

daytona
5
NYLOCABLE
IMS
REGINA
reusch
Arai
NGK
NSK
BEARINGS
JAWA
Castrol
LNK
SURFLEX
IMS

1979
500cc Jarvis/JAP Grass Tracker

J.A.Prestwich Ltd was best-known for its pre-War proprietary motorcycle engines, and after about 1950 almost exclusively made industrial motors. Since 1930, however, the ohv JAP engine had been the class leader in speedway and grasstrack, and its production and development continued well into the 1960s, when the ultimate version - the Mk4B - was finally eclipsed by newer Jawa/ESO and Weslake units. Even that wasn't quite the end, though, because in 1979-80, engineering student Mark Jarvis collaborated on the development of prototype JAP engines - about twenty of which were made - and older brother Keith fitted one into his own frame. The motors featured cutting-edge technology with four valves driven by twin overhead camshafts, and the motorcycle itself was equally innovatory, with owner-designed electronic ignition, an oil-bearing frame, and final drive via a countershaft co-located with the swinging arm pivot, which eliminated chain snatch. That meant that the usual two-speed gearbox could not be used, but in compensation the weight was reduced, and there was better drive out of bumpy corners. This unique machine showed considerable promise, but, other commitments unfortunately forced its rider and developer to retire before it was able to demonstrate its full potential.

J.A.P

JAP

J.A.P
JAP

1967
125cc Suzuki RS67

The twin-cylinder 125cc Suzuki racers of the early-1960s relied on technology gained when Ernst Degner defected from MZ, and they were undeniably effective machines. In fact, they were fast enough to give works rider Hugh Anderson the World Championship in 1963 and 1965. Nevertheless, Honda's and Yamaha's championship wins in other years indicated that Suzuki was unlikely to achieve the supremacy it wanted with a twin, so in 1967 the race shop unveiled the sensational V-four RS67. In the hands of factory rider Stuart Graham, the Museum's incredibly rare machine immediately showed its massive potential by coming second to Bill Ivy's Yamaha in the Japanese GP, despite suffering a bad start and exhaust problems. With an incredible 42bhp on tap at 16,500rpm, and a twelve speed gear box to make the best use of a respectable 1500rpm power band, the RS67 might well have gone on to dominate its class if Suzuki hadn't decided to follow suit when Honda withdrew from GP racing in 1968. Fortunately, its one and only official outing wasn't the end of the RS67's career, because one was acquired by Frank Sheen for his up and coming son, Barry, who promptly demonstrated the Suzuki's effectiveness by almost winning the 1972 World Title!

Sammy Miller Museum
New Milton Hampshire
SUZUKI RS 67 12 SPEED
125cc 90° VFOUR
42 BHP 16,500 R.P.M.
Power Band 1500
Weight 209 lbs
SUZUKI

1978
Ducati 900SS

Ducati's traditional concentration on single cylinder machines ended in 1970, when Fabio Taglioni introduced the first of the 90º V-twins that have since epitomised the marque. Ridden by Paul Smart, the new 750SS proved invincible in the 1972 Imola 200 race, and two years later an 860cc roadster won the Barcelona 24 Hour event. The best features of both machines were then combined in the range-topping 900SS production racer, which was firmly established as an all-time great when Mike Hailwood spectacularly came out of retirement to ride one to victory in the 1978 Formula 1 TT. The example seen here was made that year, and is the earliest known survivor of a small batch finished in this particular livery. It is owned by Bob Hartman who generously offered it when Ducati UK requested an appropriate machine for Sammy Miller to use in the TT Parade marking the 30th anniversary of Hailwood's TT win. A gentle parade is not in Sammy's nature, however, and in his own words he "used his trials skills to get over a wall that got in the way at Waterworks." Indomitable as ever, Sammy survived his spectacular dismount, and immediately repaired the Ducati which is now on loan to the Museum.

© Richard Dawson

Sammy 'gets a five'!!